BASIC
pumping iron

BASIC

pumping iron

Grant Breese & Dean White

MQP

About the authors

Grant Breese has worked as a Personal Trainer for five years specializing in sport specific training and rehabilitation. He has always had a passion for health, fitness, and sport, competing and working with rugby teams, athletic clubs, cricket teams, tennis players, and professional rugby players.

After a successful career in HM Royal Marines, Dean White embarked on a career of health and fitness. Working as a personal trainer, he has trained all abilities. He is a qualified fitness trainer and therapist, instructor in boxercise, coreboard, and SAQ (Speed, Agility, and Quickness).

Many thanks to Tom Henner and the Reebok Sports Club, London, for their support.

Caution

If you have a medical condition, such as high blood pressure, spinal problems, arthritis, or asthma, consult your medical practitioner or an experienced teacher before any exercise.

Published by MQ Publications Limited
12 The Ivories
6–8 Northampton Street
London N1 2HY
Tel: 020 7359 2244
Fax: 020 7359 1616
Email: mail@mqpublications.com
Website: www.mqpublications.com

Copyright © MQ Publications Limited 2004
Text © Grant Breese & Dean White 2004

Editor: Abi Rowsell
Design: Balley Design Associates
Illustrations: Oxford Designers & Illustrators
Photography: Stuart Boreham

ISBN: 1-84072-499-4
1 3 5 7 9 0 8 6 4 2

Printed in China

contents

foreword

We believe that the population as a whole needs to become more educated about all aspects of health and fitness. As we turn into a society of couch potatoes, problems such as obesity, back pain, and stress-related illnesses are becoming increasingly common.

There seems to be less leisure time than ever before, so we constantly look for quicker ways to achieve what we want: "I haven't got time to eat a proper meal so I'll drink a meal-replacement shake and take my vitamin tablets"; "I haven't got time to go to the gym to train to lose weight so I'll try the latest diets." Our obsession with trying to find short cuts has made us lose sight of how important it is to look after our health.

We are both personal fitness trainers and we come across this type of thinking every day. We spend most of our time trying to educate people about how to take better care of themselves, because even our highly motivated clients are subject to the pressures of working long hours, stress and poor nutrition and need to be reminded that fitness is about improving health first and looks second. Yet in today's world it is important to look good—and to feel good about yourself, too. We hope that by teaching you about training this book will improve both the way you look and your self-image.

It has been a privilege for us to write this book—and not just because it gives us an opportunity to reach a wider audience and have some input into the way our industry is changing for the better. We have also seen a great many people benefit greatly from doing even the most basic gym routines, and this book will, we hope, show the amazing results that can be achieved if sufficient time is dedicated to resistance training.

Grant Breese and Dean White

chapter 1
getting started

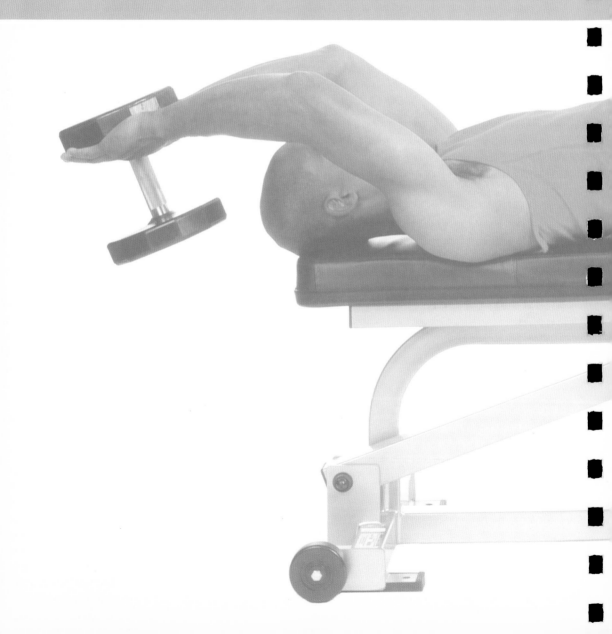

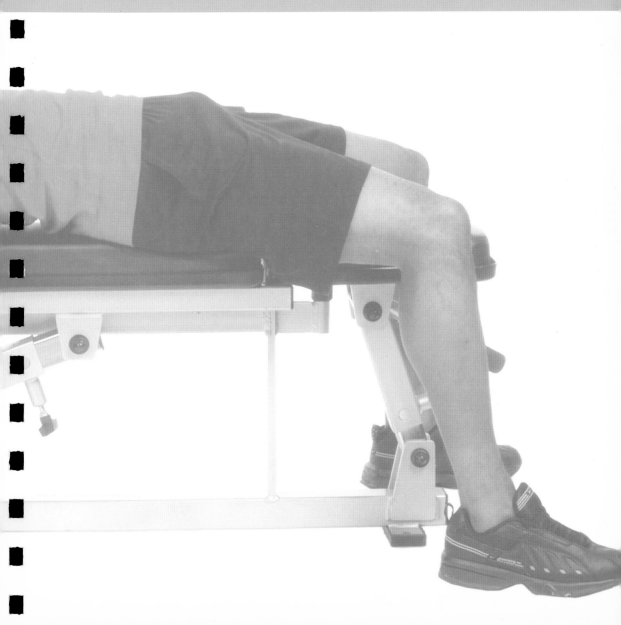

what is resistance training?

Resistance training, sometimes called weight training or strength training, is defined as a "specialized method of conditioning designed to increase muscle strength and size, muscle endurance and muscle power." It encompasses a range of techniques, such as using machines, free weights (dumbbells and barbells), resistance bands, your body weight, and cable machines.

a brief history

Today, resistance training plays an important part in all fitness programs. But this is not just a modern phenomenon. For example, Ancient Egyptian tomb paintings show people carrying out swinging exercises using stone or lead weights, and by the middle of the 16th century weight training was included in the physical education syllabus in French and German schools. It slowly became clear that resistance training had therapeutic benefits, and in 1728

below> **Resistance machines appeared in the 1970s and are now an indispensable part of training.**

John Paugh's book A Physiological, Theoretic and Practical Treatise on the Utility of Muscular Exercise for Restoring the Power of the Limb showed dumbbell exercises.

By the early 1970s, helped by the emergence of resistance machines such as the Nautilus, resistance training, and fitness training in general, had started to become more and more popular. Entrepreneurs soon spotted the trend and realized that there was money to be made in making fitness equipment and creating qualifications for fitness teachers—a multimillion-dollar industry was born. Today it is almost impossible to escape images of muscled, toned bodies in the media and the latest exercise fads are even advertised on television.

You would think that the industry would have matured by now and become more professional. In fact, it is awash with scientifically unproven exercise techniques, untested exercise equipment that it is claimed to work miracles, celebrity diets, and nutritional supplements that are said to be magic potions that will help you achieve your aims. No wonder the general public is confused—but resistance training has stood the test of time.

fundamental principles

An appropriate resistance-training program should be based on several factors: an individual's health, fitness, and goals; and a

above > **The variety of resistance machines to be found in a gym allow the modern trainer to develop a training program tailored to their own specific needs.**

correct application of the fundamental principles of training and the training environment. These principles are overload (placing a heavier than normal physical demand on muscles or muscles groups) and specificity (tailoring your individual program to your specific goals). Adherence to them, as this book shows, will lead to both structural and functional adaptations to your body as you achieve your goals.

Remember, though, that resistance training is a science-based discipline and that like all sciences it is constantly changing and developing. New training techniques and theories are always emerging and it is important to keep your exercise knowledge up to date, whichever aspect of your fitness you want to develop.

a program for success

This book will give you the basic tools to write and develop your own resistance training program—one should be part of every fitness plan, whatever your goals. Try one of the sample routines at the end of the book to get an idea of how a resistance-training workout feels, then use the information in the training principles and in the pages on body types and sets, reps, and loads to write a program for personal success.

what are the benefits of resistance training?

Resistance training has a number of clearly defined benefits. It:

■ **Increases muscle mass**

Research has shown that a standard resistance-training program—involving 30 minutes of resistance exercise three days a week—can increase muscle mass by about 3 pounds (1.4 kilograms) over an eight-week training period.

■ **Reduces body fat**

One study showed that resistance exercise resulted in the loss of 4 pounds (1.8 kilograms) of fat after three months of training, even though its subjects were eating 15 percent more calories each day.

■ **Increases metabolic rate**

Research into the effect that exercise and diet has on resting metabolic rate (RMR)—the rate at which the body burns calories while at rest—reveals that adding 3 pounds (1.4 kilograms) of muscle can increase RMR by seven percent and daily calorific requirements by 15 percent. At rest, each 2.2 pounds (1 kilogram) of muscle requires 77 kilocalories per day for tissue maintenance, so adults who have more muscles use more calories all day long and reduce the likelihood that fat will accumulate in the body.

■ **Avoids muscle loss (atrophy)**

Adults who do not resistance train lose between 4.85 pounds (2.2 kilograms) and

below > **Aerobic machines can aid strength training.**

7.06 pounds (3.2 kilograms) of muscle every decade. Although aerobic exercise improves cardiovascular fitness, it does not prevent the loss of muscle tissue. Only resistance training maintains muscle mass and strength throughout the midlife years. And when muscle is lost, the metabolic rate decreases and body fat levels and body weight slowly start to increase.

■ Increases bone mineral density
The resistance-training techniques that increase muscle strength also increase the density and mineral content of bone. Research has shown that there are significant increases in the density of the thighbone after just four months of resistance training. This helps prevent the onset of many bone problems, including osteoporosis.

■ Reduces low back pain
Extensive research into the connection between resistance training and back pain, in particular at the University of Florida Medical School, has shown that strong lower back muscles are less likely to be injured than weaker ones. A recent study showed that patients with significant low back pain found that they experienced much less pain after ten weeks of resistance training exercises designed specifically for the spinal muscles. (If you suffer from any degree of back pain you should consult your doctor before starting a training program.)

■ Improves physical appearance and posture
The abdominal and lower back muscles not only give the core of the body a powerful support structure but also dictate how you carry yourself and how you move. Resistance training can strengthen these muscles and improve your awareness of how you hold your body. The result is an improvement in your posture and your overall physical stature.

■ Gives a positive self-image and increases self-esteem
Over the last 20 years a considerable amount of research has testified to the effect that exercise has on both physical and psychological well-being. Exercise has been linked to positive changes in mood, self-esteem, self-confidence, improved satisfaction with body image and appearance, and decreased feelings of stress, anxiety, and tension. Other positive benefits include enhanced mental performance and concentration, and improvements in sleep patterns and energy levels. Exercise also has physiological effects: it raises brain levels of endorphins, the body's natural opiate painkillers, giving rise to what is known as the "runners' high."

myths about resistance training

People often become confused about training principles and practices, probably because there are so many myths about them in circulation. In our experience, the myths arise because many people lack sufficient information about exercise physiology. As a general rule, it is advisable to only believe something you hear or read in a magazine if there is scientific backing for it. Here a list of the most common myths.

■ **You can reduce fat in specific areas**
Certain exercises can improve muscle tone, but exercises cannot reduce fat in any specific area. Muscle and fat are different types of body tissue, and the body cannot directly convert one into the other. This means that exercise reduces levels of body fat throughout the body rather than only in the areas of the body you exercise. In practical terms, this means that people who have fat stomachs will not remove their fat by doing hundreds and hundreds of stomach crunches. On the other hand, aerobic exercise burns fat wherever it is and can be used to complement a resistance-training program.

■ **Your muscles will turn into fat after you stop training**
This will not happen. Muscle and fat are physiologically different and one cannot be changed into another. However, if someone trains for a time and then stops but still maintains the same calorific intake, stores of body fat, and so weight, will increase. This is because the body no longer requires the same amount of calories as were needed during training. Any calories not used to produce energy are stored as body fat.

■ **Consuming large amounts of protein or taking protein supplements will increase muscle size and strength**
Excess protein does not increase muscle growth, muscle mass or muscle strength—only correct training can achieve this. However, approximately 15 to 20 percent of total calories should come from protein-rich foods. It is a combination of a resistance-training program and a diet that contains a high proportion of complex carbohydrates that leads to an increase in muscle mass and strength.

■ **Resistance training will give women large muscles**
Because women have lower levels of the hormone testosterone than men, women cannot achieve the same levels of increase in absolute strength as men. Even programs designed specifically to increase the size of women's muscles have not had the desired results. However, the comparative success enjoyed by some female bodybuilders may be a result of:

■ genetics—higher production of testosterone;
■ extremely high volume and intensity of training;
■ rigid control of diet for increased muscularity;
■ use of banned substances.

■ **Sweating more means that body fat is being lost**
Sweating during a workout is a sign of excess body heat rather than the result of burning body fat. Even so, you can weigh less after sweating, purely because your body is losing fluid—its composition is not changing. If you

re-hydrate your body before, during and after your workout you will see that your weight is not affected drastically.

■ A vibrating belt will help abdominal weight loss

Vibrating belts are very popular. On the surface they seem to provide an attractive, quick fix for those who are not very enthusiastic about working out. Unfortunately, because muscles and skin are being manipulated passively and mechanically a negligible amount of energy is used up and there is no impact on fat loss.

below > **It is essential to have someone monitor technique if you are a beginner.**

free weights versus machines

The debate about whether it is more beneficial to train with free weights or machines has been going on for years. There are many arguments for and against, but unfortunately there are no hard and fast answers. Some people believe that the only way to make your hips and legs stronger is to use seated machine exercises; others, including us, disagree.

The only correct answer is that the choice depends on your individual circumstances. There is considerably more to take into consideration than which exercise will give the best result. You must decide which exercise will work best in terms of your physical condition and your expertise in the gym. Here are some of the pros and cons:

■ **Machines**
Machines are constantly developing. More advanced designs are being manufactured all the time with which to build the perfect body. They have a part to play at some point in every exercise program, but we believe that they should be used primarily by beginners to build strength, because machine exercises are the easiest to do—they guide your body through a motion without it having to stabilize itself.

■ **Free weights**
Free weights have been used for thousands of years. Most exercises involving them require the interaction of more muscles than are needed during machine exercises, because they require joints to be stabilized by muscles that are not always directly involved in the main movement. This allows for better and safer all-round development of both the muscle being exercised and the surrounding stabilizing muscles.

■ **Cable machines**
Cable machines are a relatively modern innovation. They enable you to incorporate considerably more stabilizing work into your program, and this can be very beneficial if you are training for a specific sport, because they allow you to copy movements from that sport. However, a cable machine's main purpose is to enhance the function of your body: you learn to make your body work as a functional unit in which all the body parts are integrated, working on specific movements rather than targeting specific muscles. And because these machines are so flexible you can adapt them to meet your specific training needs.

left > **Resistance machines are ideal for guiding the novice trainer safely through a muscle exercise.**

above > **Having a good range of free weights to choose from allows you to increase the intensity of your training as your muscle power develops.**

■ Safety considerations

It is inevitable that you will have to train alone on some occasions, even if you normally have a training partner. Some people argue that it is better to use machines when you are alone because some free-weight exercises may require the presence of a "spotter" to safeguard against injury. This can be true if you are performing each set of exercises to the point of momentary muscle fatigue. However, we believe that "know your limits" should be the watchword—regardless of how expert or inexpert you are you should have the discipline to perform your set of free-weight exercises safely without the need to have a spotter. If you feel that you are compromising your safety with a weight that is outside your capabilities you are creating a situation in which an injury may be the result.

■ The importance of variety

Being able to use both free weights and machines gives your program variety, which may be useful if you have a tendency to become bored easily and lose your motivation.

you decide

Choose your equipment on the basis of what works best for you: if you don't like free weights don't use them; if you don't like machines don't use them. Choosing your equipment does not have to be a complicated process and at this stage of your training the most important thing is to do what feels right for you.

You may have access to the best-equipped gym around, with state-of-the art machines, free weights, and cable machines, but if you do not train as hard as you can on a consistent basis you will not achieve your goals.

Remember that free weights and machines are just training tools—you need a basic knowledge of strength training to help you design the program that suits you best.

resistance training for adolescents and senior citizens

Resistance training is beneficial at any age. It helps adolescents' bones and ligaments grow and it also improves athletic performance. And strength training becomes even more important as we grow older. According to the American College of Sports Medicine (ACSM) muscle mass starts to reduce after 30, and is accompanied by a decrease in muscle density and increased quantities of fat between the muscles.

resistance training and adolescents

In this age of energy-saving devices and a TV culture, levels of activity among adolescents have declined, yet their intake of calorie-rich foods has increased. The result is that more and more young people are obese. Educating them about exercise and diet is one solution, though not the only one. It is also important that organizations that have an influence on young people encourage and motivate them to balance their interests and activities so that physical pursuits are emphasized. Here are some points to bear in mind:

■ As in all areas of fitness training, younger people should be considered as a specific group and expertise is needed when advising them about training. Safety is paramount and the anatomical and physiological implications of exercising should be considered carefully. Overall, exercising promotes the healthy development of both muscle and skeletal tissue, and the neurological and endocrinological adaptations that are caused by exercise are, respectively, beneficial to the brain and the hormonal system.
■ Muscular strength and endurance is an important consideration when working out a training program for children.
■ Moderate intensities must be used because

repetitive impact forces can cause structural damage in extreme cases.
■ Children often experience difficulty in maintaining their body temperature during exercise. Signs to watch for are changes in skin color and breathing rate, excessive sweating, and changes in mood, performance, and the ability to concentrate.
■ It is important to explain the numerous benefits of exercise to children and to reinforce the explanation regularly if they are to exercise consistently and in the long term.

resistance training and older people

Ageing is something that happens to all of us. We live in an extremely age-conscious society and the fact that examples of ageism are common helps fuel a fear of the process of growing old. Yet senior citizens can benefit greatly from resistance training, and the resulting improvements in strength and functional ability can greatly enhance the quality of life in old age. Otherwise, if muscle deterioration is allowed to go unchecked, everyday tasks can eventually start to present a daunting challenge. And it is never too late to make a start on changing your lifestyle.

Here are a number of specific problems related to ageing that can be greatly improved by regular activity and exercise:

■ **A decrease in the size of muscles and a reduced number of muscle fibers**
This is partly the result of a decrease in the number of nerve fibers, which control the muscle fibers—these tend to wither away if they are underused. However, it is mainly caused by a loss of muscle fibers as a result of inactivity—the muscle fibers are normally replaced by fat.

■ **A reduction in the number of blood capillaries**
As muscle fibers are lost, the number of the tiny blood vessels that supply them is reduced. As a result they receive less heat and energy, and this can affect their ability to stretch.

■ **Less elasticity in ligaments and tendons**
Less elasticity makes ligaments and tendons more brittle. As a result, elderly people are prone to stiffness and are more likely to be injured by sudden or violent movements.

■ **An increased risk of degenerative disorders**
Exercise protects against certain degenerative problems, such as osteoporosis, high blood pressure, and coronary artery disease.

special considerations for older people
■ For both muscular strength training and endurance training, focus on exercising the legs, hips, and pelvic areas of the body, because these are particularly vulnerable to bone fractures.
■ It is recommended that older people do eight to ten exercises that involve all the major muscle groups on at least two days a week, doing eight to fifteen repetitions.
■ Do a thorough warm-up routine and an extended cool-down routine.
■ Mobilize fingers and toes as part of the warm-up and cool-down as these are prone to arthritis.

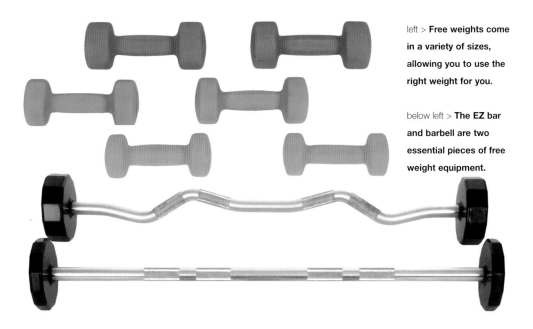

left > **Free weights come in a variety of sizes, allowing you to use the right weight for you.**

below left > **The EZ bar and barbell are two essential pieces of free weight equipment.**

weight loss and resistance training

Obesity is fast becoming a major problem in the Western world and is creating some major health issues—obese people have a higher incidence of heart disease, diabetes, hypertension, and certain types of cancer. And the ACSM defines obesity as the "percentage of body fat at which disease risk increases." It is estimated that at least one-sixth of the population are trying to lose weight at any time.

Generally, people who are trying to lose weight are encouraged to follow an aerobic-based exercise program. Such programs tend to have little if any resistance component. However, resistance training should play an important part in any exercise program designed for weight loss. With techniques such as body pump (studio-based resistance training) becoming more popular, it is now becoming more widely accepted that you do not have to spend hours on a treadmill in order to lose weight. And resistance training can be safer than cardiovascular training, which often subjects the person trying to lose weight to a huge amount of repetitive impacts—as, for example, when running on a treadmill. If you are overweight and out of condition these repetitive impacts can have disastrous effects.

Your metabolism is often the key to effective weight loss. The body is designed to run on complex or slow-releasing carbohydrates, which means whole grains, beans, lentils, vegetable, and fruits. These will produce a more consistent level of energy, relieve hunger, and also give the body more chance to use up the food for energy rather than turn it into fat. You should follow a regime of healthy eating and regular exercising and aim to lose about one to two pounds (0.5 to 1 kilogram) a week—losing more than this is more likely to be the result of loss of fluid rather than fat.

striking a balance

Successful and permanent weight loss is not just about dieting but about maintaining a well-balanced way of life

For example, most people have an imbalance of blood sugar levels at some time, probably because they eat a high-stimulant, low-carbohydrate diet. This often includes chemicals, such as caffeine and guarana, that are concentrated sources of a substance that stimulates the adrenal glands. The result is an over-production of adrenal hormones, which raise blood sugar levels—yet in the long term, fluctuating blood sugar levels can lead to problems such as diabetes. The stimulants can also lead to rapid and irregular heartbeats, headaches, insomnia and restlessness, and reduced levels of potassium, magnesium, zinc, and vitamins B and C. And over time the adrenals become weaker, resulting in persistent fatigue and tiredness.

Unfortunately, caffeine and guarana are included in many weight-loss supplements, because they can, among other effects, suppress appetite and increase the rate at which the body burns calories, both during activity and at rest. So taking them in large quantities is not a healthy substitute for a well-balanced diet and plenty of exercise.

right > **Free weights should be incorporated into any weight loss program, as lifting weights helps to improve your metabolism and general well-being.**

chapter 2
program design

principles of training

In order to put together a successful training regime you have to take into account a number of principles of training: when put into practice they form the core of any successful exercise program.

the main principles

The seven main principles are:

- frequency
- intensity
- duration
- overload
- reversibility
- progression
- specificity

Frequency

How often should you train? Or, how often can you train? There is no point setting yourself a target of four one-hour sessions a week if you know you can only manage two one-hour sessions. You should also consider how often you need to train to achieve your goals. For a beginner, three one-hour sessions a week would be appropriate to start with. As your fitness improves your frequency can increase, so long as you ensure that there is sufficient recovery time between workouts—at least a day between workouts for a beginner.

Intensity

How hard should you make your sessions? If you are a beginner you should start on the simplest exercises, because if you train too hard you run the risk of developing over-training syndrome or becoming injured.

Duration

How long will your sessions be? You need to take into account several factors that are discussed in this chapter: your body type (see pages 26–27), your training goals, your experience, and how much time you have to train. As a rough guide, a beginner should start out by training in 60-minute sessions. Construct your program accordingly.

Overload

Your body will not develop as you would like it to unless you push it beyond its current capabilities. To achieve success, you have to make the principle of progressive overload drive your training. Always work to repetition maximums and re-assess the overload at regular intervals so that training loads or weights can be increased.

Reversibility

It is easy to lose fitness that you have gained when you stop training. This concept is known as reversibility. Studies have shown that within two to three weeks of stopping an exercise program even significant fitness gains can be lost. So when you plan your program be careful not to let weeks when you cannot visit the gym—holidays, for example—interrupt your training period. "Use it or lose it," as they say.

Progression

Your body adapts to training, and the effectiveness of your training eventually reaches a plateau—when this happens you must progress your workout if you want to carry on improving. You can do this by increasing frequency, intensity, and duration of your workout and move on to more advanced exercises. If you fail to progress or you stop overloading, your increases in strength and muscle mass will flatten out, and possibly start to go into reverse.

Specificity
Your exercise program must to be tailored specifically to your goals. The more specific your program, the more likely you are to achieve what you want.

creating your program
Try the pre-planned routines at the end of this book before designing your own program. Then use the seven principles when you devise your plan. Here are some different training methods that can be used to add variety to your workouts.

Giant sets
In a giant set you exercise just one part of your body, with set one being directly followed by a set of a second exercise—as, for example, when doing Dumbbell Shoulder Presses followed by Lateral Raises.

Supersets
In a superset you perform different exercises that work two or more parts of the body—sometimes opposing muscle groups. As in a giant set, the first set is followed directly by a set of the second exercise. An example would be a set of Biceps Barbell Curls followed by a set of Triceps Assisted Dips.

Forced repetitions/assisted repetitions
In this case repetitions (reps) are performed with the help of a training partner. Once you cannot do a single more rep in a set, you ask your partner to help you do one to three more reps—the assistance provided should only be just enough for you to complete the reps.

Eccentric contractions
In this variation you continue a set until you can do no more, and then ask a training partner to help you with the concentric (up) phase (see page 34); then you carry out the eccentric (down) phase without assistance. It is important that you always carry out the down phase slowly and keep the movement under control at all times.

Drop sets
In this training method you perform a normal set with the usual weights and then follow it with a set in which you use lighter weights and do fewer repetitions. It is similar to a pre-exhaust set in which you perform a heavy set of ten repetitions, say, followed by a light set of twenty repetitions.

Circuit routine
In a circuit routine a number of exercises are performed back to back. They are performed in a set order, with a specific time or number of repetitions for each one, and rest periods are allotted between them.

Large before small

The larger muscle groups, in the back, chest, and legs, should always be trained before the smaller muscles, such as biceps and triceps. For example, if you train biceps then go on to train your back muscles you will not be able to realize the full potential of the back session. Biceps assist in most back exercises, and if your back workout starts with them already fatigued you will not be able to overload your back muscles sufficiently to produce any benefits.

body types

People often start a program without any knowledge of body types or how a certain body type responds to training and then wonder why they fail to achieve their desired goals. In order for you to get the most from your training it is important that you follow body-type guidelines, work out how your particular body will respond to resistance training and set your program and goals accordingly.

People's bodies respond differently when they undertake a weight-training program, and one reason why this should be is that people have different types of body. Generally, an individual's body type can be assessed as belonging to one of three main categories known as somatotypes. These three main body types, first described by American psychologist William H. Sheldon in the 1940s, are ectomorph, mesomorph, and endomorph, though few people fit a particular somatotype exactly. People of any body type can develop their bodies with the correct training and nutrition, but you may have to approach your training differently depending on which somatotype you conform to most closely.

- **Ectomorphs:** short upper body, long arms and legs, long narrow feet and hands, very little stored fat; this body type has a narrow chest and shoulders and long, thin muscles.
- **Mesomorphs:** large chest, long torso, solid muscle structure, and considerable natural strength.
- **Endomorphs:** short musculature, round face, short neck, wide hips, narrow shoulders, and a large amount of stored fat.

Once you have decided which category you belong to, you should follow the guidelines for your category that are given on these pages. If you find it difficult to decide, ask a friend to help you make up your mind.

ectomorph training

Ectomorphs are often referred to as "hard gainers" in the gym, and the first priority for them is to gain weight and muscle mass. They benefit most from carrying out training with heavy weights, though their progress can be slow. Strength and endurance will also need to be developed.

If you are an ectomorph, stay with more basic exercises to start with—these will enable you to lift heavier weights at low repetitions. Complete an entire training workout, but take longer rest periods. Performing such workouts using heavy weights taxes the ectomorph body and you will need to make sure you rest and recover fully between sets and sessions. Ectomorphs usually have a faster metabolism and burn their calories rapidly, so do not be concerned about cardiovascular training for the time being. You should initially concentrate on gaining lean muscle mass by doing weight training. Try to take in more calories than you are accustomed to, and if you still struggle to increase in size, try supplementing your food intake with weight-gain and protein drinks.

mesomorph training

Mesomorphs are often called "gifted ones" in the gym, as people with this body type are genetically predisposed to make large gains in their musculature. They find it easy to build muscle mass, but their program should include a range of exercises that ensure that

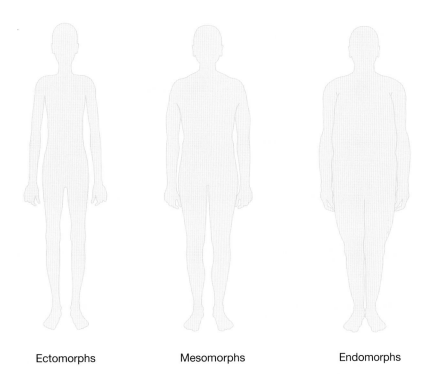

Ectomorphs   Mesomorphs   Endomorphs

their muscles develop proportionately and become shapely rather than bulky. The best results come from a combination of heavy power moves—Front Squats, Dead Lifts, and Bench Presses, for example—a variety of shaping exercises, and a more varied program overall. Mesomorphs respond extremely well to training, so over-long sessions are not needed. A balanced diet, with adequate amounts of protein and even intake of calories, is essential.

endomorph training

Endomorphs do not find it difficult to build muscle mass, and their main concern is to lose body fat and not to regain it—this can be difficult, because endomorphs are predisposed to lay down stores of body fat. Luckily, though, an endomorph's bones are wide and strong, which can be a bonus when it comes to bodybuilding. Endomorphs should therefore focus on enhancing their metabolism and performing a large number of sets with a high level of reps with short rest periods. Circuits and supersets are also beneficial, and they may also need aerobic exercise to burn off calories. The best results come if at the same time as doing their training, they adopt a low-calorie diet that contains the necessary nutritional items, such as vitamins and minerals, but the minimum quantity of proteins, carbohydrates, and fats.

muscle balance

Resistance training is an excellent way of improving strength and endurance, building bigger muscles, and improving your shape—and it can help with posture, too. The trouble is that hard work can go to waste if you do not pay attention to the principle of muscle balance—that is, of balancing the strength and size of muscles of opposing action. For example, many of our clients work on their "T-shirt muscles"—those of the chest, biceps, and shoulders—but tend to neglect their triceps and the muscles in their back and legs.

Main muscle groups (front of body)

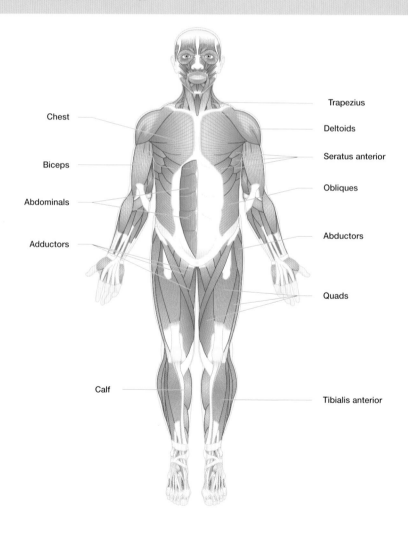

Chest

Biceps

Abdominals

Adductors

Calf

Trapezius

Deltoids

Seratus anterior

Obliques

Abductors

Quads

Tibialis anterior

work ratios

One problem is that consistently training only your "T-shirt muscles" may eventually pull your posture forward, making you round-shouldered. In the long term this can affect your lower-back strength, give rise to spinal problems, and affect your overall functional capabilities. For this reason, resistance training should also be viewed as a long-term activity, with appropriate attention being paid to muscle balance. The table on page 30 shows which muscles work in opposition over which joints, and lists the ratio to employ of exercises using them that will achieve muscle balance—this is called the work ratio. So, for example, for every three sets of leg extensions you do, you should do sets of two leg curls. Use the work ratios when designing your own program.

Main muscle groups (back of body)

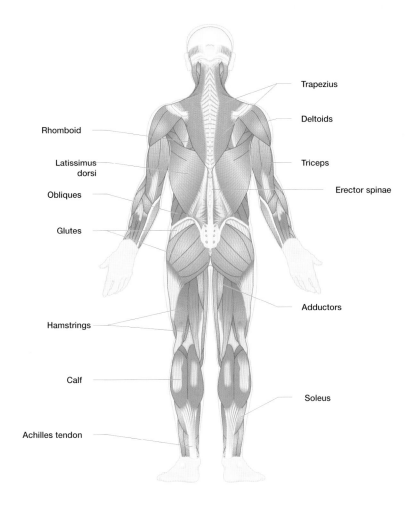

Trapezius

Deltoids

Rhomboid

Latissimus dorsi

Triceps

Obliques

Erector spinae

Glutes

Adductors

Hamstrings

Calf

Soleus

Achilles tendon

Compound and Isolation exercises

Compound exercises involve more than one joint at a time; isolation exercises involve only one joint. For example, a Barbell Squat (see page 124) involves the hip, knee and ankle joints. But an isolation exercise for the legs would be a Leg Extension (see page 115).

Examples of compound exercises
Bench Press
Barbell Squat
Military Press
Dead Lift
Assisted Pull-Up
Assisted Dip

Examples of isolation exercises
Machine Chest Flyes
Dumbbell Side Lateral Raise
Leg Extensions

Joint	Muscle groups	Ratio of sets
Knee: Extension Flexion	Quadriceps Hamstrings	3:2 *Example:* 3 x sets of Leg Extensions to 2 x sets of Leg Curls
Hip: Extension Flexion	Spinal erectors/gluteals Hip flexors/abdominals	1:1 *Example:* 1 x set of Back Extensions to 1 x set of Abdominal Reverse Crunches
Shoulders: Flexion Extension	Front deltoids Trapezius/rear deltoids	2:3 *Example:* 2 x sets of Dumbbell Front Raises to 3 x sets of Seated Low Rows
Elbow: Flexion Extension	Biceps Triceps	1:1 *Example:* 1 x set of Biceps Barbell Curls to 1 x set of Triceps Assisted Dips

the structure of a workout

Ideally, a workout should consist of the following stages: a warm-up; a stretch; a main session; a cool-down; and a period of stretching. However, this format is very rarely followed, and, unfortunately, when it is not progress tends to fall short of what it could be. Here are some questions and answers about the structure of a workout.

why do I have to warm up?

A warm-up does exactly what its name indicates: it raises the body's core temperature, mobilizes all the major joints, and increases the heart rate—all slowly. If you start strenuous exercise without a warm-up, the same things will be achieved dangerously quickly, and you will be more likely to suffer an injury. A warm-up also gives you the time to prepare mentally for the more strenuous demands of the exercises that will follow and focus on your goals for the session.

what's the best way to warm up?

Warm-ups that use all the muscles and joints are the best way of increasing your heart rate and generally preparing yourself. Brisk walking, easy jogging, and using rowing machines and elliptical trainers or cross-trainers are all effective methods.

how long should I warm up for?

There are no hard and fast rules governing the intensity or duration of a warm-up. Essentially, it depends on the individual, but anything from 5 to 20 minutes of non-intensive activity is about right—if you start to perspire lightly you have probably done enough. A typical warm-up would be to walk for two minutes, then

right> **Some gentle exercise on a running or cycling machine can be incorporated into your warm-up to gently raise body temperature and increase flexibility.**

progress to an easy jog for about three minutes, and then up the pace for the last minute or so.

when should I stretch?

You should stretch immediately after your initial warm-up and then again after your cool-down in order to increase your flexibility. Too often stretching is ignored in the fitness industry, but we believe that it is very important. It has these benefits:

- **it reduces the risk of injury;**
- **it improves mechanical efficiency;**
- **it increases the extensibility of muscles;**
- **it decreases muscle tightness;**
- **it increases relaxation and reduces stress.**

You should always perform in a slow and controlled manner, holding each position for at least 20 seconds, and never push beyond your natural range of motion. Ask an exercise specialist for help if you are unsure of the correct technique.

what does the main session consist of?

The main session is the period of the workout in which you lift and use weights or loads to induce an overload on the targeted muscle groups. This causes chemical changes within the muscles that help to make them stronger. The main session is the part of the workout in which you try to fulfill your training goals for that particular workout.

why should I cool down?

Tapering off your activity after your main session is the most effective way to finish your workout, because during it your blood has been diverted to all the working muscles and there is a tendency for it to pool in your arms and legs. A cool-down helps disperse the blood and also helps with the dispersal of lactic acid and other chemical by-products of exercise that may otherwise cause soreness in the muscles. The ideal cool-down consists of an easy, light rhythmical activity that involves the same muscles that were worked in the main session. You can even carry out your warm-up in reverse.

how long should I cool down for?

It depends on each individual and his or her fitness levels, but a cool-down can be anything from 10 to 15 minutes. Continue until you have brought your heart rate down to a comfortable level and are ready to stretch.

what if I have run out of time to cool down?

It is important that you make time for a cool-down. As well as other benefits, a cool-down helps you to wind down in a psychological sense and puts you in a relaxed frame of mind in which you can feel a quiet satisfaction that you are on the way to achieving your goals.

Stretching guidelines

Stretching is more important at the end of an exercise session than after the warm-up, so if you are short on time go straight from the warm-up to the main session, then cool down and stretch.

- Always breathe calmly and rhythmically.
- Stretch with the back supported where necessary.
- Try and hold each stretch for at least 20 seconds and as much as 60 seconds.

sets, repetitions, and loads

The most effective way to train muscle groups is to use a certain range of repetitions in conjunction with a specific load or weight, to take the correct amount of rest between sets of exercises (sets), and to perform each at the correct speed (the tempo). In order to work out what loads/weights, sets, and reps to use for an exercise, select a weight, try the exercise using the appropriate number of reps, then adjust it on the next set if necessary until you reach your ideal range.

What your ideal range of reps is, and what weight you choose, also depends on what you want to get out of resistance training.

For example, if you can bench-press 55 pounds (25 kilograms) for ten reps comfortably but your goal is strength training, you should increase the load or weight slightly. This is because you are training in the bodybuilding repetition range at this weight. So you should gradually increase the load/weight above 55 pounds (25 kilograms) until you can bench-press for a maximum of six reps using suitable sets and taking appropriate rest periods.

training goal categories

The chart below lists the different training goals and type of training that each one demands. Use it as a guide to working out your ideal range of reps—taking into account the other factors discussed in this book—so as to achieve your goals time-effectively.

Strength: a strength-training program involves high-resistance, near-maximum effort for a small number of reps with a full recovery period between sets.

Power: this program increases power, defined as "the optimal combination of speed and strength to produce movement." It is especially useful for explosive sports.

Bodybuilding: a bodybuilding program involves using loads or weights moderate enough to allow more reps. It increases overall muscle size and can help sculpt the body.

Muscle endurance: in this program muscles contract over a large number of reps with very little recovery allowed between each set. The relative intensity is low but the overall volume is very high. It helps in endurance events that require more stamina than strength.

Training goals	Sets of exercises	Repetitions	Rest period	Load/weight
Strength	2–6	< 6	2–5 minutes	Just enough to perform 2–6 reps—heavy
Power	3–5	1–3	2–5 minutes	1–3 reps—very heavy
Bodybuilding	3–6	6–12	30 seconds–1.5 minutes	6–12 reps—moderate
Muscular endurance	2–3	> 12	< 30 seconds	More than 12 reps—light

tempo

Your tempo—the speed with which you perform an exercise—is an important consideration when planning a workout, though many people give little thought to it.

three phases

Each rep consists of three phases, representing three different types of action—eccentric, isometric, and concentric—and the tempo given for it establishes how long each phase should last. For example, when you perform a bench press: first, you lower the bar to your chest (this is the eccentric phase); then you hold the bar for a second (the isometric phase); and finally you push the bar away from your chest and back toward to the start position (the concentric phase). Let us look at what is happening during these phases of a bench press in more detail.

eccentric action

This normally takes place when a weight is being lowered in a controlled way and the muscles being used are lengthening—muscles can only shorten or lengthen. In the majority of exercises, gravitational pull helps you return to an exercise's starting position. However, it is important that the bar's descent is closely controlled.

isometric action

This occurs when a muscle is activated and acquires force but there is no movement at a joint—an isometric contraction takes place to hold the weight in place. For example, in the case of a Bench Press you hold the bar above your chest before starting to push it back up—there is no movement, but your muscles are working hard to keep the bar in place.

concentric action

This occurs when the muscles being used are contracting, and is the ideal time to apply maximum effort.

timing

Ideally, it should take around 2 to 3 seconds to perform the first phase of the exercise, then there should be a short pause before returning to the start, which should take another 2 to 3 seconds. Overall, then, a rep should take 5 to 7 seconds if it is to be effective and safe (the exception is when you are specifically training for speed, perhaps to help sporting performance).

In this book, tempo is expressed in the "2:1:2" form. This indicates that the first phase of the movement (concentric or eccentric, depending on the exercise) should take 2 seconds; the second phase (isometric) should take 1 second; and that the final phase (concentric or eccentric) should take 2 seconds. Different exercises demand different tempos.

how much is enough?

If you do too many training sessions of excessive intensity and content too often, and give yourself insufficient rest and time to recover, it is likely that you will develop over-training syndrome, also known as "staleness." People often ignore the problem, but if you are one of them you will risk damaging your health.

It is easy to recover from the syndrome if you learn to recognize its signs and take action—then you can make yourself fit and healthy again within a few days. The key to recovery is to make sure that you have sufficient rest and food, and that you are properly hydrated. You should also avoid any strenuous activity until you have recovered completely, otherwise you risk weakening your immune system and setting your recovery back. Here are some of the telltale signs of over-training syndrome:

- decreased performance
- increased muscle soreness
- decreased body fat
- lethargy
- altered sleeping patterns
- general physical weakness

periodization

One way of avoiding over-training and also keeping positive about your training goals is known as periodization—a concept that is often discussed by fitness professionals but rarely put into practice day-to-day in the gym. It involves setting your goals and dividing them into short- and long-term ones. You can break them down into blocks that last for a year, a month, a week, or just an individual session.

The classic periodization model does this in terms of a "macrocycle," "mesocycles," and "microcycles." Typically, a macrocycle covers an entire year of training, though it could cover six months, say. Within the macrocycle are two mesocyles, each lasting anything from several weeks to several months—precisely how long depends on the nature of your goals and the length of you macrocycle. Each mesocycle contains two or more microcycles, which are normally one week long but can last up to four weeks.

Periodization, when integrated with program design and goal setting, is an excellent motivator, and also gives your goals structure and direction.

muscle soreness

Sometimes your muscles may feel sore after your first resistance-training program. It is not known exactly why this happens, but it is possible that overloading the muscles causes micro-tears and damages the muscle fibers. The problem is more acute for beginners.

A problem known as delayed onset of muscle soreness (DOMS) can become apparent between 24 and 48 hours after exercising, and it may last up to ten days. The severity and location of the discomfort varies according to which muscles have been worked.

The way to avoid these problems is to make a slow transition from a sedentary lifestyle to one that incorporates active exercise. Achieving this will also make your training experience not only enjoyable but long-term and goal-oriented. Listen to your body, make sure you take adequate rest and recovery between sessions, eat healthily, and train to the best of your ability.

chapter 3

mind and body

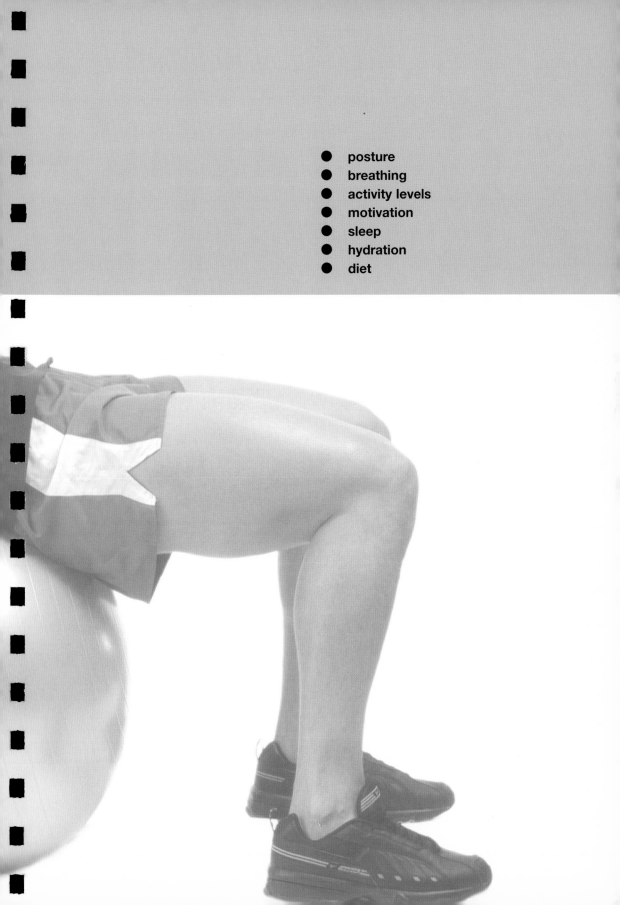

● posture
● breathing
● activity levels
● motivation
● sleep
● hydration
● diet

posture

"Posture is the relationship or alignment between different body parts. A person's posture is the foundation for movement and, like a house, if the foundation is poor the whole body will suffer," said the famous physiotherapist Chris Norris.

Poor posture can result in a range of soft tissue and joint problems, the most common of them being low back pain. Research indicates that as many as 80 percent of people in the Western world will suffer at least one disabling episode of low back pain during their lives; and that, at any one time, as many as 35 percent of the population suffer from some degree of back pain.

One reason is that, whatever your job, the chances are that you spend much of your time putting your posture to the test. If you sit at a desk, the height of your chair, the position of your computer, and even how you use your telephone can all affect your posture. If you have a manual job, you may be putting your

posture at risk by continually bending over or repeating the same movements over and over again. The only way to avoid developing problems is to make absolutely sure that your working environment is as friendly to your posture as possible, and to keep your posture in mind at all times.

Correct posture when you are training is just as important as it is during day-to-day life. You should always keep in mind what position your body is meant to be in, and never compromise it by attempting to lift weights that are too heavy for you—remember that posture and technique are everything.

One reason for this is that exercising with poor posture can increase your chance of

Neutral spine exercises

This neutral spine exercise should also be attempted both sitting and lying down, using the same guidelines.

- Set your head by retracting your chin in and back until your ears are in a line over the top of your shoulders; the distance between your earlobes and shoulders should increase.
- Set your shoulder girdle by opening your chest and retracting your shoulderblades in toward the spine. Pull your shoulderblades down toward your pelvis.
- Set your pelvis by drawing your abdominal muscles in, allowing it to move up at the front (a pelvic tilt).
- Set your feet by positioning them a shoulder-width apart with your toes facing forward and tighten your buttocks.

injury as well as preventing you from getting the maximum benefit and development from what you are doing.

posture, spinal problems, and the neutral spine

The stresses that modern life places on our posture have resulted in three spinal problems becoming increasingly more common. These are: lordosis, an accentuated inward curve of the spine in the lower back; kyphosis, an accentuated outward curve of the spine in the shoulder region (a variation on kyphosis is the sway back posture, in which the hips push forward); and scoliosis, a curvature of the spine to one side of the body or the other. All these spinal problems give rise to back pain and increasingly serious problems.

Ideally, the spine should be held in what is known as the neutral position (see box, left, below)—and at some points in this book we will ask you to set it in that position.

Lordotic posture: there is excessive extension in the lower back—the lumbar spine— as a result of a lengthening of the abdominal and gluteal muscles and a shortening of the muscles that flex the hip.

Kyphotic posture: the upper part of the spine is flexed forward, there is compression in the neck joints, and the shoulders, the chest muscles are tight, and the lower trapezius is lengthened.

Sway back posture: the hips are pushed forward because the hip flexors are lengthened and there is very little curve in the lower back; the shoulders are dropped and move forward.

breathing

You might be thinking, "Why do I need to learn about breathing?" After all, breathing is something that we all do naturally, without any thought, throughout our lives. But the problem is that most people breathe incorrectly, and even more people breathe incorrectly when they are taking exercise.

The most common type of faulty breathing is chest breathing. The diaphragm is the most important muscle in respiration, and most chest breathers under-utilize it. Instead, they overwork their accessory respiratory muscles, in the ribs and chest, often as a result of stress, bad posture, or because it has become a habit to do so.

It is easy to spot a chest breather: the chest rises during most of the time that a breath is being taken in (the inspiration phase of breathing). In correct, diaphragmatic, breathing, the chest should only rise during the last third of the inspiration phase.

It is vital that you breathe correctly during exercise, because incorrect breathing does not deliver oxygen to your muscles in sufficient quantities to cope with the demands you are making of them.

practicing diaphragmatic breathing

The easiest way to learn how breathe with your diaphragm is to practice when lying flat on your back. Once you have mastered the technique, you can move on to practice diaphragmatic breathing when seated, and then when standing.

■ Take up the starting position (flat on your back, seated or standing).
■ Place your hands on your abdomen or hold a water bottle on top of it, so that you can either feel or see your abdomen moving.

■ Slowly inhale through your nose, trying to push your abdominal muscles out as you do so. Feel the movement with your hands or watch the bottle rise, but make sure that you do not allow your chest to expand.
■ Exhale through your mouth, slowly letting your abdomen fall back.

breathing during exercise

It is often hard to remember to breathe correctly while you are exercising, especially when exercises demand that you inhale or exhale at certain specific stages. Nevertheless, it is vital for the effectiveness of the exercise that you breathe correctly, using your diaphragm. As to when you should inhale or exhale, here is the golden rule:

during every exercise, regardless of what type of equipment you are using, you must always breathe out at the same time as you make the greatest effort.

You should be able to sense which part of any movement demands the greatest effort if you tune into what you are doing and listen to your body. With practice, it becomes fairly easy to exhale and inhale at the correct times. There are two exceptions: if you are nearing exhaustion at the end of your set you may find it a struggle to perform the last part of a movement without holding your breath; and it may also be difficult if you are performing any short, explosive movement.

a breathing variation

Normally, when employing diaphragmatic breathing, you push your abdominal muscles out when you inhale, and let them fall back when you exhale. However, during certain exercises in this book you will be asked to actively draw your abdominal muscles in, as if drawing your navel into your spine, at the same time as you exhale.

First of all, practice this variation on diaphragmatic breathing when you are lying flat on your back, then move on to trying it both when seated and when standing—eventually you should be able to do it even when you are walking. The more you practice the technique the easier it will become to apply it during an exercise.

why should I pull in my abdomen?

Imagine that your trunk is a cylinder. As you draw your abdominal wall in toward your spine, the cylinder's walls are pulled in and the diaphragm lowers, compressing it from the top. This increases the pressure (it is called intra-abdominal pressure) inside the cylinder and makes it more solid. As a result, your trunk is more able to resist the external stresses that are placed upon it during exercise. This means that the risk of injuring your trunk or lower back is lessened. However, this exercise does need to be practiced in order to strengthen the muscles involved so that your back has more protection when you are lifting heavier loads.

activity levels

How active are you? Do you spend six to eight hours sleeping, an hour traveling to work, anything from eight to ten hours sitting at your desk, an hour traveling home, a few hours watching television, and then do you go back to bed? If so, you are spending a considerable amount of time sitting or lying down—but you share a lifestyle that is common to many of us in modern-day society. Unfortunately, it is a lifestyle that not only causes postural problems, but also piles on the pounds.

moderate and vigorous activity

Even 30 minutes of moderate activity, undertaken three to five times a week, can decrease your risk of developing coronary heart disease and osteoporosis, and boost all the positive side-effects of activity, such as a feeling of physical well-being, improved self-esteem, relief from mild depression, increased confidence, increased expenditure of calories, enhanced energy levels, and an increased resting metabolic rate—which means that you burn more calories even when you are at rest. Strangely, regular moderate activity also decreases your appetite. Here are some examples of moderate activities:

- cycling
- brisk walking
- mowing the lawn
- playing badminton
- a leisurely swim

Of course, you will burn off even more calories, and benefit from the positive effects of activity to an even greater degree, if you undertake more vigorous exercise, especially on a regular basis.

Examples of more strenuous activities include:

- running
- racquet games
- circuit training
- hill walking
- stair climbing

metabolic rate, resistance training and weight loss

Your resting metabolic rate (RMR) normally accounts for between 60 and 75 percent of your daily expenditure of calories. One of the benefits of resistance training is that, in the long term, it can not only increase RMR but also increase your body's fat-free mass (FFM). If an effective, goal-based resistance training program is coupled with an appropriate calorie-based diet you can lose weight and increase your FFM by increasing your body's lean muscle mass. To be effective, your program must involve working all your major muscles during two training sessions a week at a moderately high intensity.

So you do not have to be a fanatic about training to get into shape. Your metabolism, or, rather, the changes that training can make to it, can make all the difference and help your body become leaner and you to become fitter.

Exercise can have an even more powerful effect on your resting metabolic rate if you structure your resistance training and set goals for it in the way outlined in this book. Remember, too, that the effects of exercising are cumulative, and that moderate exercise can actually decrease your appetite. Normally those who do not exercise have larger appetites, with the effect that the pounds creep on, slowly but inexorably.

motivation

Resistance training is demanding, both in terms of time and effort. You have to be well-motivated to persevere with your program, yet, surprisingly, many people overlook the question of motivation when designing their programs—and, as a result, give up on them. There are various ways of improving motivation, but most of them require input from a specialist. However, here are some guidelines.

motivational questions

There are three main sets of questions whose answers will affect your motivation to persevere with an exercise program: personal questions, which have to do with your perceptions of exercise; program questions, which have to do with your exercise program, its convenience and the enjoyment you derive from it; and environmental questions, which concern the external world that you can, and, at times, cannot control.

Personal questions include:

- how do you feel about the value of exercise?
- what is your past experience with exercising?
- what is your personal motivation level?
- is your exercise program convenient and enjoyable?
- do you have the ability to resolve any obstacles that may hinder your exercise plans, such as, travel problems, illness, and time constraints?

Program questions include:

■ Is your program convenient, when you take into account the time of day you intend to train, the number of sessions you have decided to undertake, the flexibility of your schedule, and the accessibility of your training facilities?

■ Does your chosen activity require any type of preparation that is special, costly, or takes too much time?

■ Is your program sufficiently intense that you find it challenging, but not too intense that you find it punishing?

■ Is your program sufficiently varied that it will maintain your interest?

Environmental questions include:

■ Are you comfortable with the location in which workouts take place?

■ Have you set yourself some regular cues—leaving your gym kit packed by your front door, for example; or scheduling workouts into your diary—in order to remind yourself to follow your program?

■ Do you have an ongoing support system? Have you told your family and friends what you are doing; do you have a training partner; have you made friends with the fitness staff at your gym to encourage them to give you advice and answer any questions that you may have?

setting goals

The most sensible way of setting goals is to follow **SMART**: **S** for Specific; **M** for Measurable; **A** for Attainable; **R** for Realistic; and **T** for Tangible.

Specific: a goal that is specific has a much greater chance of being achieved than a general one. A general goal would be, "I want to get bigger." Make this goal more specific by

saying, "I want to put on 11 pounds (5 kilograms) of muscle." Try to set yourself a sensible time-frame.

Measurable: establish criteria by which you can measure your progress toward attaining each goal that you set—for example, the amount of weight you put on weekly and monthly, and your quarterly body measurements. Measuring progress constantly helps you stay on-track and focused, and gives you the satisfaction of seeing how you are gradually realizing your goals.

Attainable: identify the goals that are the most important to you and think about the ways and means that you can use to make them come true. Think about the process you will have to go through—how many times a week will you have to train? How much time do you have available for training? Are the goals that you have set yourself achievable? All these questions need to be answered when you set out your goals.

Realistic: your goals must be realistic in order for you to achieve them. This may sound very obvious, but you will soon feel the pressure to give up if you do appear to be getting close to the goals you have set yourself. Your goals must also be achievable in physiological terms, so consult an exercise specialist to make sure that your goals are not unrealistic—setting yourself a goal of putting on 22 pounds (10 kilograms) of muscle in a week, for example, is wildly unrealistic.

Tangible: a goal can be considered to be "tangible" when you can appreciate that it has been realized by using one of your senses. You should choose a goal that you can taste, touch, smell, see, or hear.

Build on success—start with small goals that lead to larger ones.

Be realistic—set attainable goals. Being realistic will prevent you from becoming frustrated later on.

Set well-defined goals and reward yourself for reaching them—this will encourage you to set new goals.

Keep a journal—you will be able to see how far you have progressed and evaluate what worked best for you.

Take bimonthly photos—these will allow you to see changes over time; often the changes occur gradually and are difficult to see from day to day.

Create variety—add new exercises once you have learned the basics.

Do not make exercise just another item on your to-do list—try to get really involved with what you are doing and connect with it on a deeper level.

Educate yourself—the more you learn the less likely you are to become injured or become stuck in a rut.

Know your limits and stay within them—fatigue, insomnia, and irritability are all signs of over-training.

sleep

The third of your life that you spend sleeping can have a significant effect on the other two-thirds of your life. Sleep is a necessity, not a luxury, and the average adult is genetically programmed to require about eight hours of quality sleep a night (though this varies from person to person).

Sleep-deprivation can impact negatively on your everyday life. It can lead to:

- reduced alertness
- mood swings
- a decrease in your general levels of health, and, in particular, to the health of your immune system
- a reduction in creativity
- decreased productivity

There are five distinct stages of sleep, and we cycle through them every 90 minutes or so.

Stage 1

This can last between 10 seconds and 10 minutes, and is normally the transition period between being awake and asleep, when you can be woken easily and are often still very aware of where you are.

Stage 2

This usually lasts between 10 minutes and 20 minutes, and is characterized by a reduction in muscle tension, heart rate, and breathing rate. At this stage, you could still be just as easily woken but may feel disorientated, slightly drowsy and not completely aware of your immediate suroundings.

Stage 3

This is a short transitional period between stage 2 and stage 4, in which a distinct reduction in brain-wave activity can be seen on an electroencephalograph (EEG), which can be used to monitor brain waves.

Stage 4

This stage is sometimes referred to as "delta sleep," because of the slow delta waves that can be seen on an EEG. It is a regenerative phase, in which your body heals, repairs, grows, and restores itself. Muscle relaxation is complete, blood pressure, heart rate, and respiration slow, and body temperature is reduced to save energy and fight infections.

Stage 5

This stage is often referred to as the "rapid-eye-movement" or REM-phase of sleep, and you are the most likely to dream during it. The mind is extremely active and usually your eyes move about rapidly during this phase. Your heart rate increases and your breathing becomes irregular. The brain also occupies itself during this time by taking the chance to sort out its files, and this facilitates the storage and retention of memories and the organization of information.

When breathing and heart rates eventually normalize, you may awake with a sudden start, and may even vaguely remember a dream for a few brief moments. After the first REM period, you return to stage 2 of sleep. The cycle normally lasts for up to 90 minutes in total, until you wake up naturally or are woken up by some outside event.

hydration

It is vital that you keep your body in an adequate state of hydration, not only when exercising, but during day-to-day life. This is because certain chemical reactions that play an essential part in the metabolism can only take place if the temperature of the body is kept within a narrow range.

Ideally, you should drink between four to six US pints (2 to 3 liters) of water every day, depending on your daily levels of general activity, how much you exercise and at what intensity and for how long, and your intake of other liquids.

Sweating is an effective way of controlling body temperature when heat starts to build-up as a result of activity, but is only effective for so long as sufficient fluid is available. If there is insufficient fluid, and you are dehydrated, your exercise performance will decline and you will

take longer to recover. Here are some signs that you have become dehydrated:

- **a dry mouth**
- **feeling thirsty (when this happens it is a sign that you are already about 10 percent dehydrated)**
- **a dry skin**
- **a decreased output of urine**
- **dark-colored urine**
- **a loss of performance**
- **slurred speech**
- **lethargy**

Here are some ways to guard against dehydration:

- drink fluid frequently, throughout the day
- ensure you have a bottle of water at your place of work and at home
- carry a small bottle with you, especially if you are traveling on public transport
- remember that both caffeine and alcohol have a dehydrating effect

fluid and electrolytes

The body can survive for about four weeks without food, but for only four to ten days without water. This is not surprising, because water is the largest component of the body, representing between 45 and 70 percent of your body weight—about 75 percent of muscle tissue is water, and water makes up about 20 percent of fatty tissue. But water does not just form a major part of the fabric of the body and play a vital role in heat regulation: it contains the essential electrolytes sodium, potassium, and chloride. These are essential to muscle contraction and the conduction of electrical impulses along nerves. Any disturbance in the balance of these electrolytes in body fluids is likely to interfere with your performance—yet the main electrolytes lost when you sweat are sodium, chloride, and potassium. So the message is crystal clear: keep yourself adequately hydrated at all times.

Homemade sports drink

A useful homemade sports drink can be made from:

- 8 US fluid ounces (250 milliliters) of your favorite concentrated fruit juice.
- 17 to 25 US fluid ounces (500 to 750 milliliters) of water.

diet

Muscle is an active tissue in the body, and even when it is at rest it needs to burn calories just to survive. And since resistance training increases the amount of calories required during rest—the resting metabolic rate—an adequate supply of calories becomes essential. But where these calories come from is important, too.

Our bodies are made up of billions of individual cells, and each group of cells has a different function to perform—ultimately their functions interlock to sustain life. But cells demand fuel, and this is why we have to eat. To put it into the simplest terms, every morsel of food that we eat feeds our cells.

So what you eat is vitally important to your health. And the extra demands for calories, and so for food, that resistance training makes both when you are exercising and when you are at rest make the quality of your diet even more important. Strangely, though, dietary considerations are often overlooked in the fitness industry. This is a pity, because eating a good, well-balanced diet can help you achieve your goals more quickly.

Understanding what a healthy diet consists of is not an easy task, however, because much of the advice that you read in newspapers and magazines is conflicting, confusing, and even downright misleading.

Essentially, there are six main nutrient groups that should make up our daily food intake, all in varying quantities. They are:

- Carbohydrate
- Protein
- Fat
- Vitamins
- Minerals
- Water

Use the food pyramid below to construct your own dietary plan for health and exercizing.

A guide to daily food choices

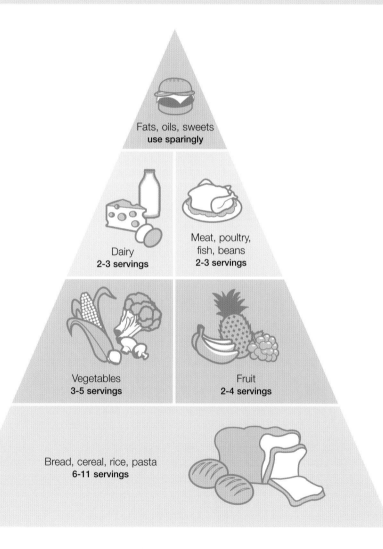

Fats, oils, sweets
use sparingly

Dairy
2-3 servings

Meat, poultry, fish, beans
2-3 servings

Vegetables
3-5 servings

Fruit
2-4 servings

Bread, cereal, rice, pasta
6-11 servings

shoulders

● **machine exercises 50–52**

machine shoulder press

machine lateral raise

machine shoulder press

beginner/intermediate

benefits This is a very good strength exercise that can also build a good base level of muscle in the shoulder region. Because there is a fixed plan of motion, little technical ability is needed to make the exercise effective. A great all-round shoulder exercise.

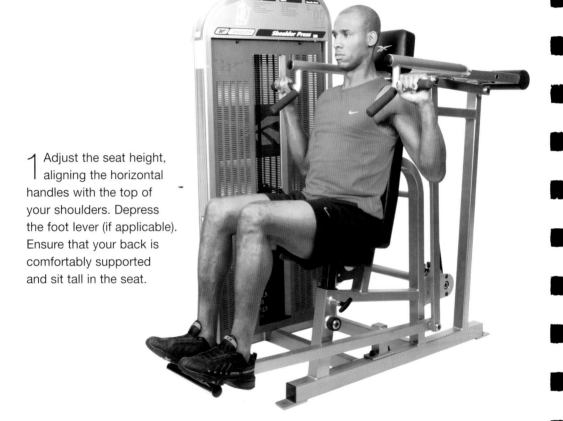

1 Adjust the seat height, aligning the horizontal handles with the top of your shoulders. Depress the foot lever (if applicable). Ensure that your back is comfortably supported and sit tall in the seat.

precautions

■ Ensure that your posture is correct and, in particular, that your lower back is supported adequately and that your back does not arch too much.

■ Using too much weight too soon will compromise both your form and, possibly, your safety.

2 Push up, extending your arms over your head in a controlled manner. Avoid any snapping or locking out of the elbows.

variation

■ Use the vertical grip (where applicable).

3 Return to the start position in a controlled way and complete the remainder of your reps.

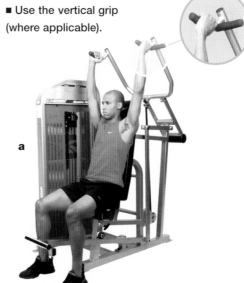

a

machine lateral raise

beginner

benefits This exercise isolates the medial head of the shoulder, but because its movement is fixed there is little room for error. This makes the exercise an ideal one for beginners.

1 Adjust the seat height so that the center of your shoulder aligns with the machine's rotational axis.

2 Keeping your back tall, brace your shoulders and lift your arms to the horizontal while keeping your shoulders down. Maintain correct posture.

3 Return your arms to the starting position, keeping the movement under control.

variation

- Vary the height to which the arms are raised—if you go beyond shoulder level it usually means that you hit more traps than if you stick to the conventional range.

precautions

- Reduce the weight if your posture or technique cannot be maintained for the correct range of reps.

cable side lateral raise

beginner/intermediate

benefits This is an excellent exercise that isolates the medial head of the deltoids (at the side of the shoulders) almost completely. The movement is very effective and beginners and those at intermediate or advanced levels can use it as part of a shoulder workout.

1 Stand close to the cable machine and side-on to it, position your arm slightly in front of your thighs and take hold of the handle.

variation

■ Progress to using dumbbells, with two arms together at the same time, or try the exercise when seated.
■ The higher your arms are raised the more the traps become involved and the less work there is for your deltoid muscles to do.

precautions

■ Start with a light-to-moderate weight, keeping good form and maintaining your posture throughout.
■ Always bring your arm to the horizontal position, or even slightly above shoulder height, but maintain a slight bend in your elbow.

2 Inhale and, keeping a slight bend in the elbow, raise your arm out to the side of the body until your upper arm is level with your shoulder. Keep your palm facing down.

3 Slowly, and with the movement under control, lower your arm back down to the start position.

cable rear lateral raise

intermediate

benefits This exercise works the deltoids, in the shoulder, especially the rear head of each deltoid. At the end of the movement, when you pinch your scapulae (shoulderblades) together, you can emphasize trapezius and the rhomboids (in the back).

1 Kneel down on your hands and knees side-on to the cable machine, making sure that you keep your back straight and your abdominal muscles pulled in. Reach through and grab the handle, then take up the slack on the weight stack.

precautions

- Use a very light weight at first, as it is very important that you keep perfect form without cheating during the movement.
- Where possible, use a mirror to check the position of your back throughout your set.

2 Keeping your elbow slightly bent, pull your arm back through until your upper arm is in line with your shoulder. At the same time extend your lower arm and contract the rear of your shoulder.

3 Keeping the movement under control, guide the cable back to the start position, keeping the tension on throughout, and repeat for the desired number of reps.

variation

- Use dumbbells in a bent-over standing position—using two arms at the same time.
- Do the exercise using dumbbells while seated.
- Do the exercise in a prone position on an incline bench.

rotator cuff—internal

beginner/intermediate

benefits This exercise helps prevent injuries to the shoulder girdle and is very effective. It works the small but important internal rotator-cuff muscles beneath the shoulder muscles. Doing this exercise is an ideal way of finishing a shoulder workout or a rehab routine.

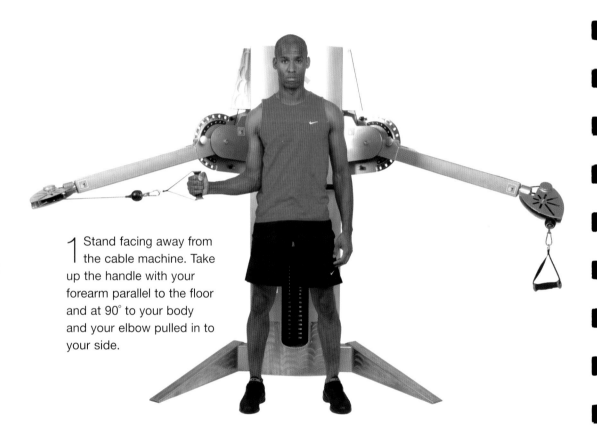

1 Stand facing away from the cable machine. Take up the handle with your forearm parallel to the floor and at 90° to your body and your elbow pulled in to your side.

precautions

- Use a very light weight until you can perform the movement perfectly, with little or no bouncing or momentum changes.
- Keep the tempo slow and controlled and make sure you use your full range of movement.

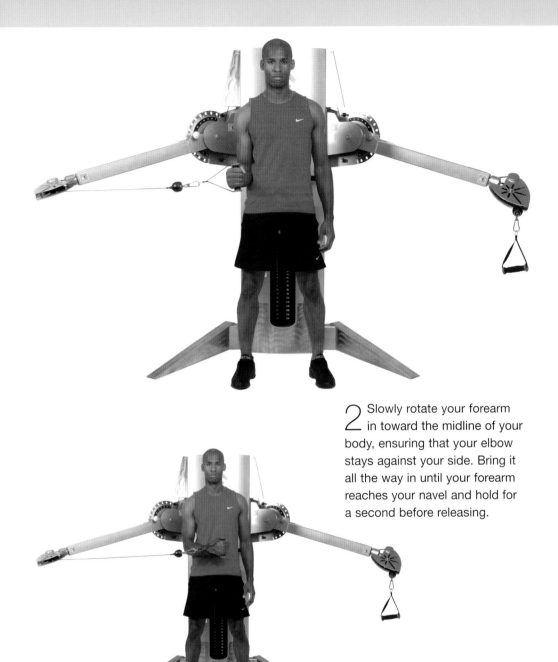

2 Slowly rotate your forearm in toward the midline of your body, ensuring that your elbow stays against your side. Bring it all the way in until your forearm reaches your navel and hold for a second before releasing.

3 Keeping the movement under control, release back out to the start position. Make sure that the movement is strict with no jerking and that you do not cheat by using other muscle groups.

variation

■ Use dumbbells while lying on your side—either on the floor or a bench.

rotator cuff—external

beginner/intermediate

benefits As with the internal rotator-cuff exercise, this exercise helps prevent injuries to the shoulder girdle, and is extremely effective. It works the external layer of rotator-cuff muscles beneath the shoulder muscles. Doing this exercise is an ideal way of finishing a shoulder workout or a rehab routine. In conjunction with the internal rotator cuff-exercise it plays an important part in the wind-up of a shoulder workout or rehab routine.

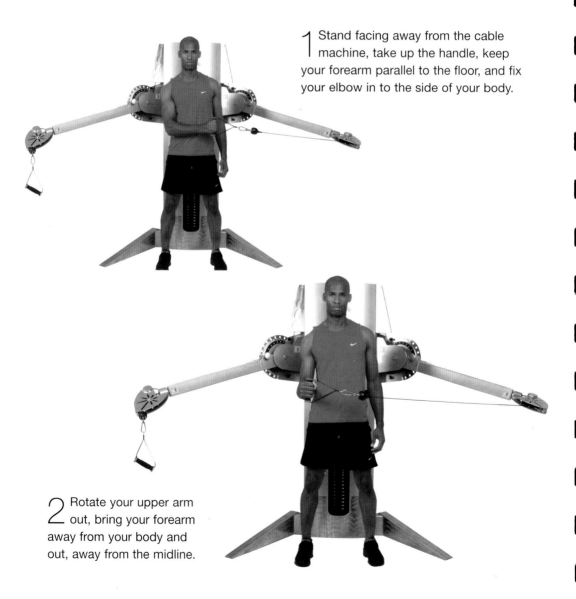

1 Stand facing away from the cable machine, take up the handle, keep your forearm parallel to the floor, and fix your elbow in to the side of your body.

2 Rotate your upper arm out, bring your forearm away from your body and out, away from the midline.

3 Take the handle out to the side as much as possible within
your own range of motion, and hold for a second before
bringing it back in toward your navel.

variation

■ After you have perfected the cable
machine exercise, try using a light
dumbbell while lying on your side on a
bench or on the floor.

precautions

■ Keep your elbow pivoting from your
side—this will make sure that all your
efforts are focused on the shoulder's
rotator-cuff muscles.
■ Start by using a manageable weight
with which you can perform the
required number of reps.

bar military press

beginner/intermediate

benefits This is one of the most effective of all the shoulder-building exercises, and should be incorporated in workout programs of all levels once the correct movement has been mastered and feels comfortable.

1 Sit with your back on a bench that allows a steep incline—between 80° and 90°. Grasp the barbell with an overhand (pronated) grip with your hands just a little wider than shoulder-width apart and rest it on your upper chest.

2 Brace your shoulders and back, then inhale and press the bar straight up, keeping your elbows slightly bent at the top.

3 To finish, lower back down to the start position, keeping your abdominals and lower back braced, then repeat for the desired number of reps.

variation

■ Do the exercise when standing—it requires more abdominal and lower back strength than when seated (a, b).
■ Use dumbbells and press them either together or alternately.
■ If your shoulder flexibility allows, press the barbell from behind your neck— you will need several months of basic conditioning work before you can do this.
■ Vary the distance between your hands on the barbell, up to 6 inches (15 centimeters) wider than shoulder-width.

a

b

bar upright row

beginner/intermediate

benefits This exercise works not only the shoulders but the trapezius (in the back), making it a good linking exercise between shoulders and back.

1 Stand with your feet slightly wider than a shoulder-width apart and take an overhand grip on a barbell with your hands also a shoulder-width apart.

2 Pull up to the level of your chin, keeping the bar close to your body and keeping your elbows higher than the bar.

3 Hold for a few seconds before lowering back to the start position, ensuring that your elbows remain slightly bent and avoiding any bouncing or jerking movements.

variation

■ Pulling the bar slightly higher will work the trapezius muscles more.
■ Vary the hand-widths—when they are closer together more emphasis will be placed on the trapezius muscles and when they are wider, more on the shoulder muscles.
■ Try using dumbbells once your shoulder strength has reached a reasonable level—pull two up to chin level at the same time.

precautions

■ Keep your knees slightly bent, taking the strain off the joints.
■ Pull in your abdominals and brace your upper body before moving the bar up toward your chin.
■ Keep your elbows higher than the bar at all times.

dumbbell lateral raise

beginner/intermediate

benefits This exercise is almost identical to one given as a variant to the Cable Side Lateral Raise (see page 53), but in this case the exercise can be changed slightly to incorporate either more or less work for the upper back by using varying ranges of motion.

1 Stand with your feet a shoulder-width apart, keeping your back straight and arms slightly in front of your torso. With your elbows slightly bent, take a dumbbell in each hand.

precautions

■ Never use heavy weights as doing so will affect your performance and could increase the risk that you suffer a shoulder injury.
■ Always use the correct technique and never "cheat" the weight up.

2 Raise the dumbbells out and up to the level of your shoulders. Keep your palms facing the ground.

3 Keeping your elbows bent, lower slowly back to the start position and repeat for the desired number of reps.

variation

- Vary the starting hand positions: in front of the torso (a); behind it (b); and at the sides.
- Try the exercise when seated and when standing, and when using one arm at a time—in the latter case, brace yourself by holding on to an upright bench with your free hand.

a

b

chest

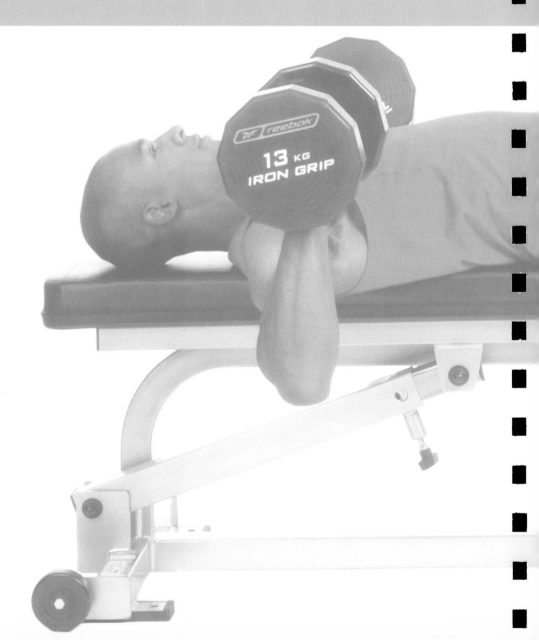

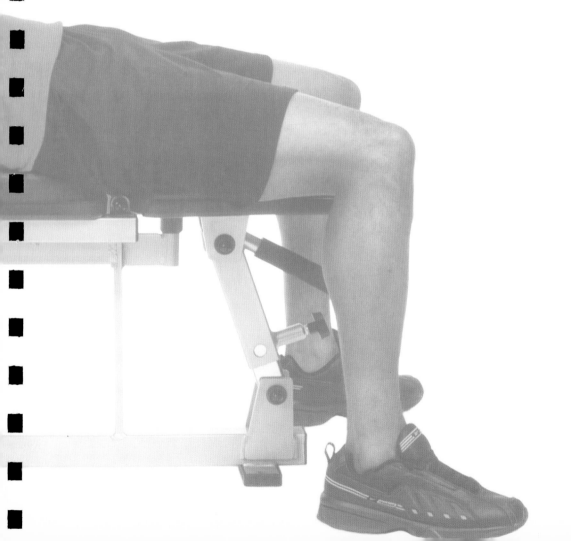

machine chest press

beginner/intermediate

benefits This is a good, basic chest exercise that is ideal for building basic upper-body strength, especially in the front of the shoulders and triceps muscle in the upper arm.

precautions

- Ensure that your shoulders are relaxed throughout—let your arms do the work.
- Your back should be pulled in to the seat at all times and your breathing should be relaxed—exhale when pushing the handles forward.
- Decrease the weight if you cannot maintain correct posture.

1 Adjust the seat height so the handles are in line with your mid-chest area.

2 Keeping your wrists, elbows, and shoulders in a line, push forward, extending your arms and keeping your back straight against the seat.

3 Do not snap your arms out—instead, keep a slight bend in your elbow when your arms are at their full extension.

4 Return to the start position, keeping the movement under control and maintaining the alignment of your wrists, elbows, and shoulders. Aim to feel a slight stretch in the chest area when returning back.

variation

- Use the horizontal and vertical handles (if there are any).

machine chest flye

beginner/intermediate

benefits This is a good finishing exercise that can also be used to isolate the chest muscles. It works within a fixed range of motion so there is little chance that any errors will creep in or any injury occur.

1 Adjust the seat height so that your upper arms are parallel to the floor. Depress the foot lever (if necessary) and grasp the handholds, pushing your forearms into the pads.

2 Keeping your back straight, sit tall and brace your shoulders and chest, and keeping the movement under control bring your arms together in front of your chest until the pads meet.

3 Hold for a second, contracting your chest, and then return to the start position, with the movement under complete control, and repeat for the desired number of reps.

precautions

- Avoid excessive stretching of your chest and shoulder area.
- Work within a comfortable range of motion.
- If you cannot maintain your posture, decrease the amount of weight.

cable crossover

intermediate

benefits This is a very good exercise for helping to shape the chest, and is also a good way to finish off a chest workout. You can work different areas of your chest by varying the tilt of your upper body.

1 Stand with your feet slightly wider than a shoulder-width apart with your back facing the cable machine. Select a light weight, grasp the handles and then bend at the waist, keeping your arms out to the side of your body with your elbows slightly bent.

precautions

■ Maintain perfect posture throughout and always keep your abdominal muscles and lower-back muscles pulled in tight.

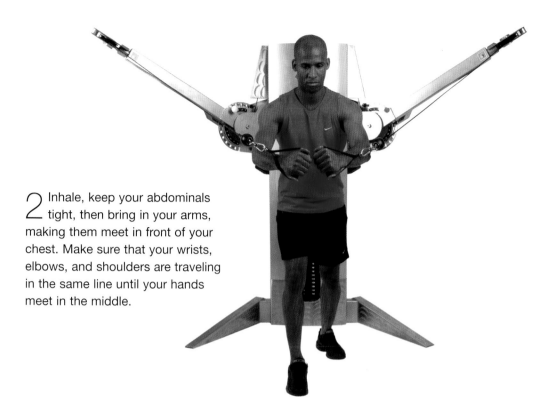

2 Inhale, keep your abdominals tight, then bring in your arms, making them meet in front of your chest. Make sure that your wrists, elbows, and shoulders are traveling in the same line until your hands meet in the middle.

3 Hold for a second and squeeze your chest. Then, keeping the movement under control, ease your arms back to the start—stretch your chest, making sure that your shoulders are relaxed and your back is straight.

variation

■ Try crossing your hands over in front, or make one higher and the other lower when your hands are down in front of your chest.

cable chest press

intermediate

benefits This exercise is similar to other bench and chest presses but the unstable nature of cables makes it a little more advanced than them. The comparative lack of stability means that there has to be more emphasis on working not just the major chest muscles but also the muscles that assist them.

1 Lie back on the bench with your feet on the ground or any foot platform, grasp a cable handle in each hand, and extend your arms up above your shoulders.

2 With your palms facing each other, inhale and slowly lower the handles out and down to the sides of your torso. Make sure that your wrists are straight and your elbows are in line with your shoulders.

3 Perform a full stretch in the lower position, then exhale and push back up into the start position, keeping your wrists, elbows, and shoulders in line.

4 During the lowering phase, rotate your hands so that your palms face down toward your feet when the move has been finished—rotate your hands back as you push back up.

variation

- Try doing this exercise on a declining or inclining bench to work different areas of your chest.
- Try using one arm at a time in order to work more abdominal and lower-back muscles.

precautions

- If you find that you cannot maintain the correct form, decrease the weight level until you can—otherwise you may be at risk of an injury.

cable chest flye

intermediate

benefits This movement is a good one for shaping the chest, and because cables are being used there is constant tension on the muscles. However, it is a little too advanced for a beginner and should be regarded as a progression from Machine Chest Flye (see page 67) once basic strength has been built up.

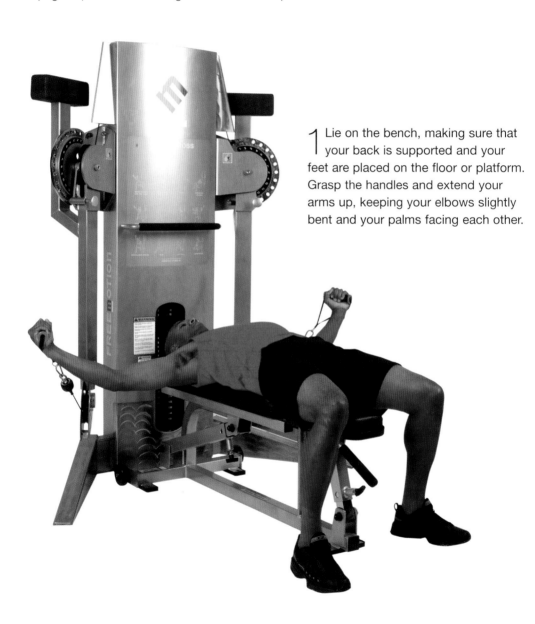

1 Lie on the bench, making sure that your back is supported and your feet are placed on the floor or platform. Grasp the handles and extend your arms up, keeping your elbows slightly bent and your palms facing each other.

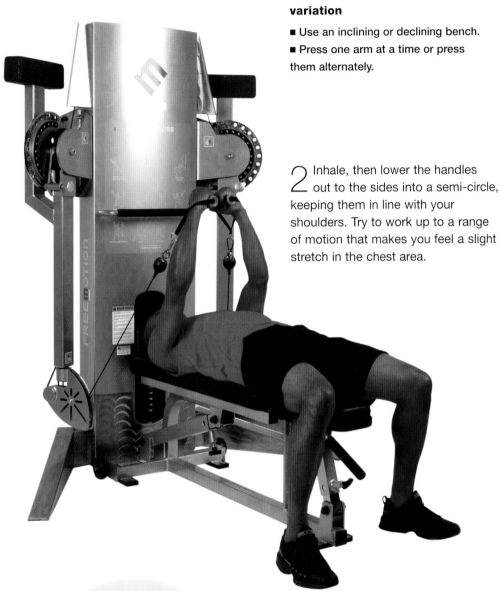

variation

- Use an inclining or declining bench.
- Press one arm at a time or press them alternately.

2 Inhale, then lower the handles out to the sides into a semi-circle, keeping them in line with your shoulders. Try to work up to a range of motion that makes you feel a slight stretch in the chest area.

precautions

- Make sure that your lower back is supported throughout the exercise.
- If your technique starts to fail, make sure that you reduce the amount of weight being used.

3 Exhale and bring the handles back into the midline of your body, with your elbows still slightly bent, and contract the chest for a second time. Repeat for the desired number of repetitions.

barbell bench press

intermediate

benefits This exercise is excellent for building strength and muscle mass, but it is not suitable for a beginner—it should be regarded as a useful progression from Machine Chest Press (see page 66). It works on the front of the shoulders and triceps as well as the chest.

1 Lie on your back with your feet supported either by a raised platform or the floor. Make sure that you do not over-extend your lower back and keep your buttocks in contact with the bench. Take an overhand grip on the bar, slightly wider than a shoulder-width apart. Inhale and push the bar off the rack (if there is one) then move it lower down to the midline of your chest.

precautions

- If your lower back over-extends and feels uncomfortable, bend your knees and raise your legs off the ground. Keep your hips and knees at 90°, with both your feet and knees together.
- Make sure that you do not snap your elbows at the top of the press. If you keep your elbows slightly bent the stress at the joints will be relieved.

2 Try to keep the bar, your wrists, elbows, and your shoulders working on the same line of axis—straight up and down.

3 Hold for a second then push the bar back up, making sure that your shoulders do not hunch forward away from the bench and that it is your triceps muscles and chest that are pushing.

4 Keep your upper body in contact with the bench as much as possible and keep your breathing rhythmical—exhale when you push the bar back up.

variation

- Try bench presses on inclining and declining benches.
- Once you can do bench presses confidently, progress to using dumbbells. You need slightly more control with these, but there is an increased range of movement (a, b).

a

b

dumbbell flye

intermediate

benefits This exercise isolates the chest and can also help with flexibility. However, it should not be used with heavy weights or undertaken by beginners, because of the stress that it places on the shoulder girdle.

1 Grasp a light-to-moderate pair of dumbbells, then lie back with your arms extended up over your upper chest. Your elbows should be slightly bent and your arms facing each other.

precautions

- Make sure that your lower back does not become over-extended or arch to compensate for using too much weight.
- Keep your shoulders relaxed and in contact with the bench—do not round your shoulders off at any point.

2 Inhale, then slowly lower your arms out to the sides of your torso in a semi-circle—keep the movement under control with your elbows still slightly bent—until there is a full, comfortable stretch in the area of your chest and shoulders around the level of shoulder-height.

variation

- Try using inclining and declining benches to work different areas of your chest.

3 Hold the stretch for a second before bringing the dumbbells back in to meet at the top of the movement—exhale as you return to the starting position.

dumbbell pullover

intermediate

benefits This exercise develops the entire chest and also works the triceps muscles and back muscles. It is a good linking exercise between a chest workout and a back workout.

1 Lie on a flat bench with your head supported and your feet either in contact with the floor or a raised platform. Hold a dumbbell with both hands, encircling it with your palms against the underside of the top set of plates. Raise the dumbbell up in front of your chest, with your elbows slightly bent.

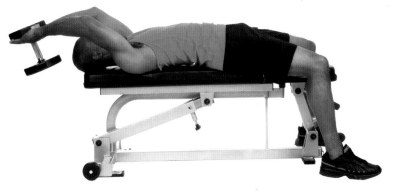

2 Inhale and lower the dumbbell back past your head and back to the limit of your range of motion, keeping your elbows slightly bent at all times. Hold the stretch for a second before exhaling and returning the dumbbell back up to the starting position.

3 Repeat for the number of repetitions desired, maintaining correct posture.

precautions

- Work within a comfortable range of motion and use less weight if your posture is less than perfect.
- Keep your elbows slightly bent and in close to the sides of your torso throughout the exercise.

variation

- Do the exercise with a barbell.
- Try using a bench with a slight incline if the flexibility of your shoulder or back is a little restricted.

chapter 6

back

- **machine exercises 80–83**
  assisted pull-up
  machine lateral pull-down

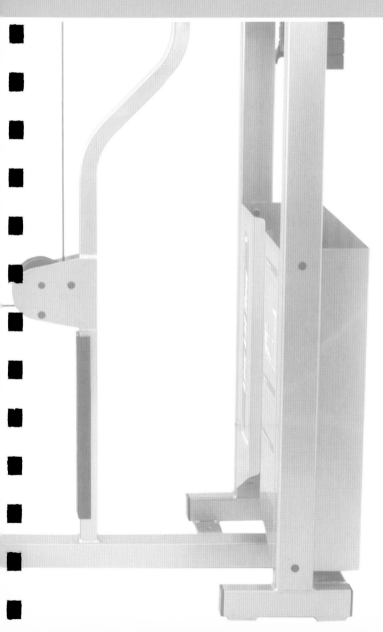

assisted pull-up

beginner/intermediate

benefits This is an excellent exercise for the whole back that can be performed by people of any ability. It also works the biceps muscles and forearm muscles very effectively, so it can be used as part of an arm workout.

1 Choose a suitable weight, then kneel or stand on the platform and grip the handles. Keep your abdominals and lower back muscles strong and slowly extend your arms until they are fully stretched. Make sure that you keep your shoulders down and retracted slightly back—this will help to keep the tension on your back muscles.

2 Keeping the movement under control and your elbows pulled down and back, pull yourself back up to the start position. Repeat for the desired number of reps.

variation

■ Use different hand positions to work different parts of the back muscles and shoulder muscles: try parallel (a) and underarm (b).
■ Change the width of your hands: start with a shoulder-width grip, then a slightly wider one, and then a closer one.

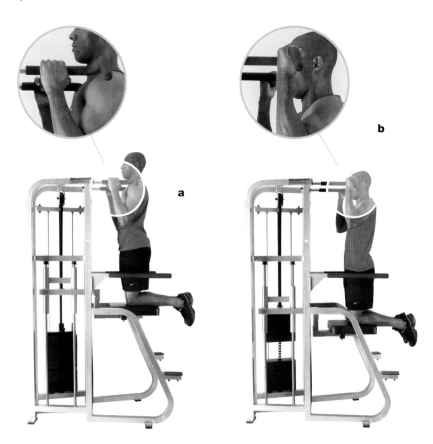

precautions

■ If your technique starts to fail, make sure that you reduce the amount of weight being used.

variation

■ Use an inclining or declining bench.
■ Press one arm at a time or press them alternately.

machine lateral pull-down

beginner/intermediate

benefits Like the Assisted Pull-Up (see page 80), this exercise not only works the back muscles but also the biceps muscles and the muscles of the forearms, improving the strength of your grip. It is a good exercise for beginners because it allows them to build up strength before progressing to body-weight pull-ups and chin-ups.

1 Adjust the kneepads to comfortably support your legs and to help stabilize your upper-body. Choose a suitable weight then stand up and grip the bar with your hands a shoulder-width apart before pulling the bar back down and taking your place under the knee support.

2 Stay seated and extend your arms up and above your position, then pull the bar down until it reaches your upper chest.

precautions

■ Do not use heavy weights too soon or you may be at risk of injury.
■ Let your arms and back muscles do the work—pull your elbows back and down during the exercise.

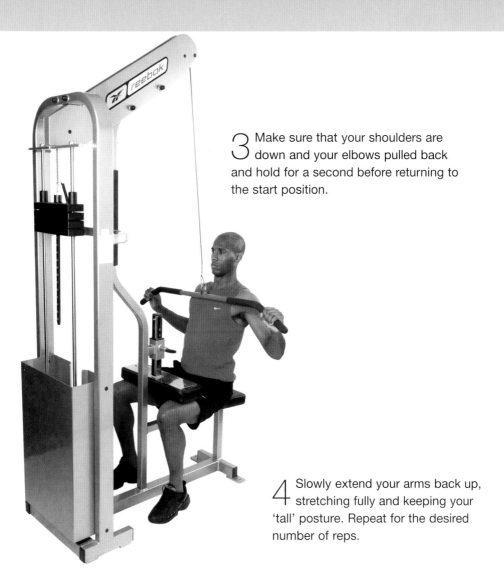

3 Make sure that your shoulders are down and your elbows pulled back and hold for a second before returning to the start position.

4 Slowly extend your arms back up, stretching fully and keeping your 'tall' posture. Repeat for the desired number of reps.

variation

- Change the angle of your upper body when pulling down by leaning back slightly more. Maintain your 'tall' posture, though, and do not hunch forward.
- Try using a close underarm grip (a, b)—doing this makes your biceps muscles work harder during the exercise—or make your hands slightly wider than a shoulder-width apart in order to work the back a little more.

a

b

cable seated low row

beginner/intermediate

benefits This is very good back exercise that also isolates the upper back effectively when you retract the shoulderblades during the movement. The eccentric part of the movement also stretches the back muscles out.

1 Place your feet on the platform, keeping a slight bend in your knees and making your posture "tall." Grasp the handles and extend your back forward while keeping your shoulders slightly retracted, and then pull your elbows in and back toward the sides of your torso— the handle should come all the way in until it reaches your navel.

2 Hold the position for a second before returning back out, keeping the movement under control: your arms returning to the extended position; your back going slightly forward; and with your knees slightly bent.

3 Repeat for the desired number of reps.

variation

■ Try using different handles: rope, V-grip, or the Machine Lateral grip.

precautions

■ Maintain your "tall" posture throughout the exercise. Reduce the amount of weight you are using if you cannot do so.
■ Keep your elbows pulled in close to your upper body to ensure that your back muscles are working hard.

cable straight arm pull-down

beginner/intermediate

benefits This exercise works the back well and the triceps muscles assist with the movement. The exercise should not be performed using heavy weights as doing so will compromise its effectiveness.

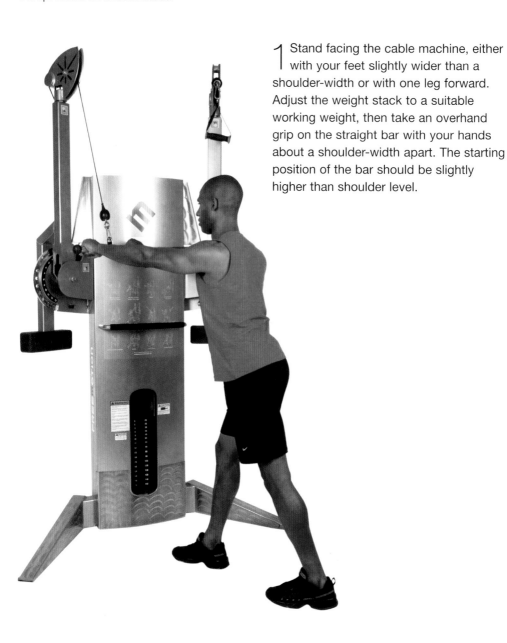

1 Stand facing the cable machine, either with your feet slightly wider than a shoulder-width or with one leg forward. Adjust the weight stack to a suitable working weight, then take an overhand grip on the straight bar with your hands about a shoulder-width apart. The starting position of the bar should be slightly higher than shoulder level.

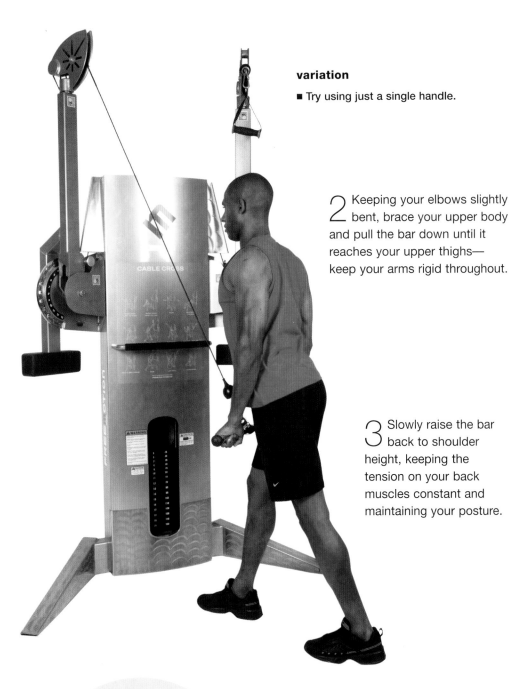

variation

- Try using just a single handle.

2 Keeping your elbows slightly bent, brace your upper body and pull the bar down until it reaches your upper thighs—keep your arms rigid throughout.

3 Slowly raise the bar back to shoulder height, keeping the tension on your back muscles constant and maintaining your posture.

precautions

- Keep you abdominal muscles drawn in and your back motionless throughout.
- Start with a light-to-moderate weight on this exercise—form is very hard to maintain unless you do so.

cable seated high row

beginner/intermediate

benefits This simple but extremely effective exercise works the back muscles that also help with posture. It is vital both that correct posture is maintained and that the weights used are not too heavy.

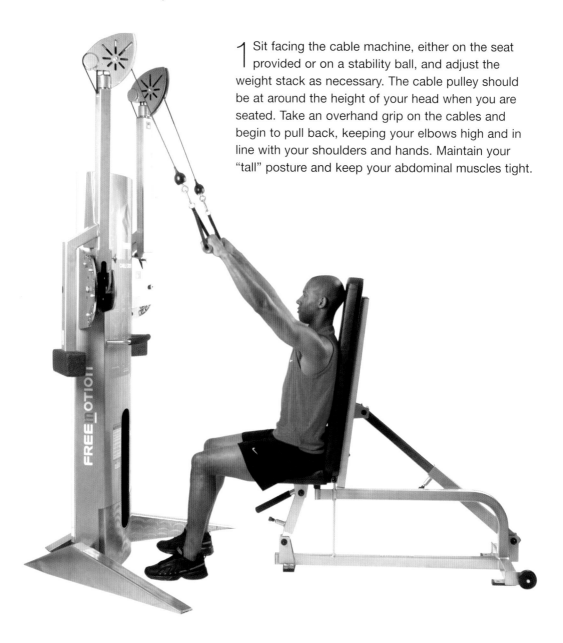

1 Sit facing the cable machine, either on the seat provided or on a stability ball, and adjust the weight stack as necessary. The cable pulley should be at around the height of your head when you are seated. Take an overhand grip on the cables and begin to pull back, keeping your elbows high and in line with your shoulders and hands. Maintain your "tall" posture and keep your abdominal muscles tight.

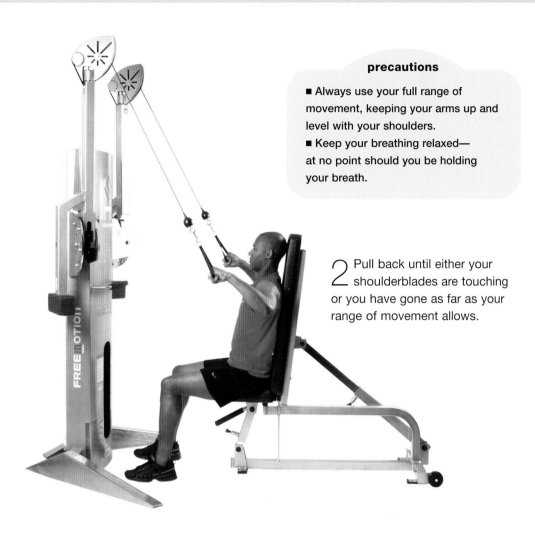

precautions

- Always use your full range of movement, keeping your arms up and level with your shoulders.
- Keep your breathing relaxed— at no point should you be holding your breath.

2 Pull back until either your shoulderblades are touching or you have gone as far as your range of movement allows.

3 Retract and hold for a second before easing back to the start position, ensuring that your wrist, elbows, and shoulders are traveling in the same line. Repeat for the desired number of reps.

variation

- Once you have mastered this exercise, progress to doing it when standing (a, b)—this requires more core stability in the abdominal and lower-back areas.
- Try using just one arm at a time— this also requires slightly more strength in your core areas.

a

b

bar bent row

intermediate

benefits This exercise works the back as well as, indirectly, your biceps muscles and forearms. Correct posture is essential and only intermediate trainees should attempt the exercise, unless under the supervision of an exercise specialist .

1 Standing with your knees slightly bent, bend at the waist at an angle of about 45°, keeping your back straight. Take up your grip on the bar with your hands slightly wider than a shoulder-width and your arms hanging straight down from your shoulders.

precautions

■ It is very important to keep your back straight throughout this exercise, so make sure that your posture is perfect before you start to add more weight to the bar.
■ Work within your movement range to maximize muscle growth.

2 Inhale and brace your core areas, then pull the bar straight toward your navel until it touches your midsection. Your elbows should be pulled back in close to your torso.

3 Return to the start position, keeping the movement under close control. Repeat for the number of reps required.

variation

■ Change hand positions: try wide, close, underarm, and overhand.
■ Vary your body angle from 35° to 70°, bending only at the waist.

biceps

preacher bench biceps curl

beginner

benefits This is a basic but effective exercise for beginners that builds up the size and strength of your biceps muscles.

variation

- Use one arm at a time.

1 Sit with your chest against the chest support, keeping your back straight with your arms over the front of the pad and your arms facing up. Grip the handles, keeping your arms parallel to each other, and make sure that you are comfortable before you start the exercise.

2 Exhale, slowly pulling the bar toward your shoulders by bending at the elbow but with your arms staying parallel and your shoulders still. Raise the bar as close to your shoulders as is comfortable, inhale and slowly return to the starting position.

precautions

- Do not let your shoulders rise and fall when performing the pulling movement.
- Maintain good body position throughout the movement and keep the movement under control, regardless of the tempo you choose.
- Keep your feet in contact with the floor.

standing cable biceps curl

beginner/intermediate

benefits Varying your hand position during this exercise, which also puts more emphasis on stability, can help promote a better all-round development of biceps. And as the cables work independently you can also correct any strength imbalance between your two biceps.

1 Stand tall with your feet a shoulder-width apart and your knees slightly flexed rather than locked, and hold the cable handles by your sides with your palms facing out in front of you.

2 Pull the cables slowly toward your shoulders as you exhale, bending at the elbows but keeping them still. Make sure that your starting body position does not change at all.

precautions

■ Make sure that there is no movement in your torso—you should not push your hips forward or swing forward and back.

■ Make sure that you do not allow your elbows to travel forward as you pull your hands upward.

3 Pull your hands as close to your shoulders as you can without letting your elbows travel forward.

4 When the up-phase has been completed, inhale and slowly lower your hands back to the starting position.

variation

- Vary the grip to focus on different areas of your biceps (a, b, c, d).
- Try to perform the exercise when sitting on a bench or a ball.
- Exercise each arm alternately.

dumbbell biceps curl

beginner

benefits This is a useful exercise for beginners because it helps correct any imbalance between the strength of the two biceps and allows for variations of hand grip that help develop biceps further.

1 Stand tall, maintaining good posture, with your feet hip-distance apart, and your knees slightly flexed, leaving your arms by your sides with your palms facing forward.

precautions

- Maintain good posture throughout the movement and make sure that only your forearms move.
- Do not allow your elbows to travel forward or push your hips forward during the movement.
- Use a mirror to check on your technique and body position.

2 Inhale, then raise the dumbbells slowly toward your shoulders as you exhale, keeping your elbows close to your sides. Make sure that you do not allow your elbows to travel forward.

3 When you have raised the dumbbells to your shoulders inhale and slowly lower them back to the starting position.

variation

- Try doing the exercise using a reverse grip (a, b) and then a hammer grip (c, d).
- Try doing the exercise when sitting on a bench or a ball.
- Use your arms alternately.

a   b   c   d

ez bar standing biceps curl

beginner/intermediate

benefits This is a useful exercise that allows you to lift heavy weights and increase the size and strength of your biceps muscles. Experimenting with variations on the handgrip can help all-round development.

1 Stand tall with your feet a shoulder-width apart and your knees slightly flexed. Work your hands from the ends of the bar toward the middle, gripping the bar at the first bends you reach.

precautions

■ For the best results, maintain a good body position and do not allow any movement of your torso or elbows.

2 Inhale, then slowly raise the bar toward your shoulders as you exhale, keeping your elbows close to your sides without letting them travel forward.

3 Inhale and slowly return the bar to the starting position.

variation

■ Try the exercise with an overhand grip (a, b).
■ Change the position of your hands on the bar, using a wide grip or a narrow grip.

a

b

triceps

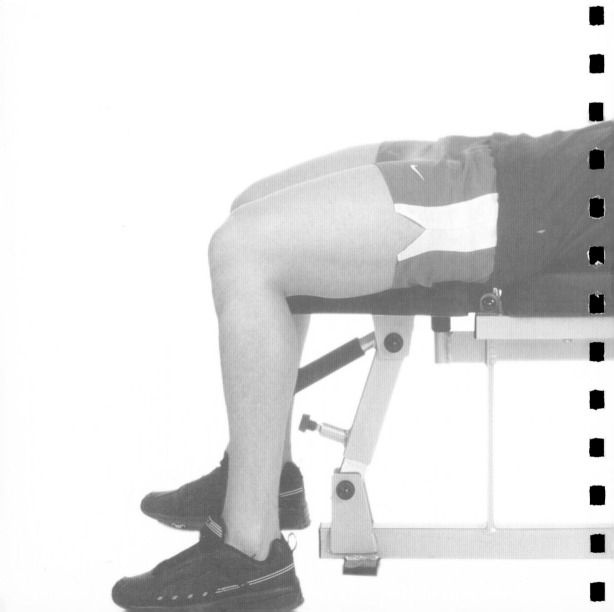

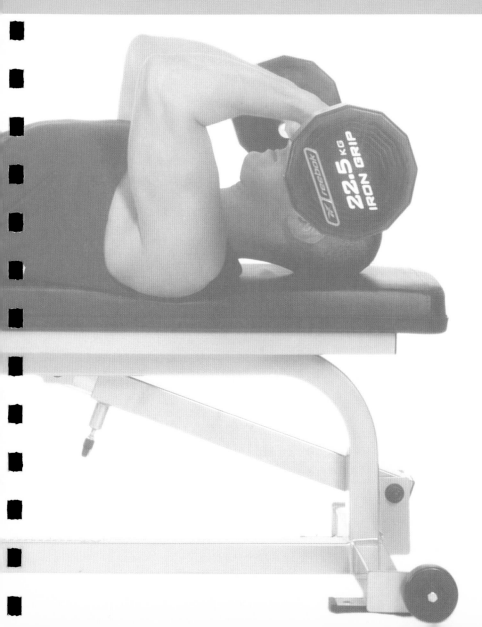

machine triceps extension

beginner

benefits This is a simple beginner's exercise that allows you to lift heavy weights and gives your triceps muscles a good all-round shape.

1 Adjust the pad to support your chest. Sit with your chest against the pads and bring the handles up. Grasp the handles with your palms facing each other and arms parallel to each other, resting the back of your arms on the chest pad. Maintain a straight back by pushing your hips toward the back of the seat.

precautions

■ Do not allow your elbows and upper arms to rise off the chest pad on the return phase of the exercise.

2 Without letting your shoulders rise, and keeping your arms parallel to each other, exhale and push the handles down and away from you.

variation

■ Try exercising a single arm at a time.

3 Push until your arms are straight, then inhale as you slowly return to the start position.

triceps assisted dip

beginner/intermediate

benefits This triceps exercise can require considerable strength when the assist is not used. It also works the pectoral muscles of the chest to some degree.

variation

- As your strength increases, lessen the assisting weight.
- As a progression, and if you are sufficiently strong, try pushing just your own body weight.

1 Place a hand on each handle, keeping your hands in line with your elbows and shoulders. Slowly place first one and then the other knee onto the kneepad.

2 Lower your body weight gently onto the kneepad, keeping your shoulders, elbows, hips, and knees in line.

precautions

- Select a weight that enables you to complete the exercise comfortably until you become completely familiar with the movement.
- Do not let your head come forward or your shoulders shrug during any part of the movement.
- Avoid snapping your elbows at the top of the movement.

3 Inhale as the kneepad lowers and push your elbows out behind you. Lower yourself down to a comfortable position, but aim to have an angle at 90° at each elbow.

4 When you have reached the position, exhale and slowly push yourself back up to the start position.

cable triceps push-down

intermediate

benefits This is a slightly more advanced exercise in which you can vary your grip to help with all-round development. It also helps develop good stability when standing.

1 Stand tall, facing the cable machine with your feet hip-distance apart, your knees slightly flexed, and your elbows pulled back and tucked into your sides. Hold the handles in an underhand grip with your palms facing up.

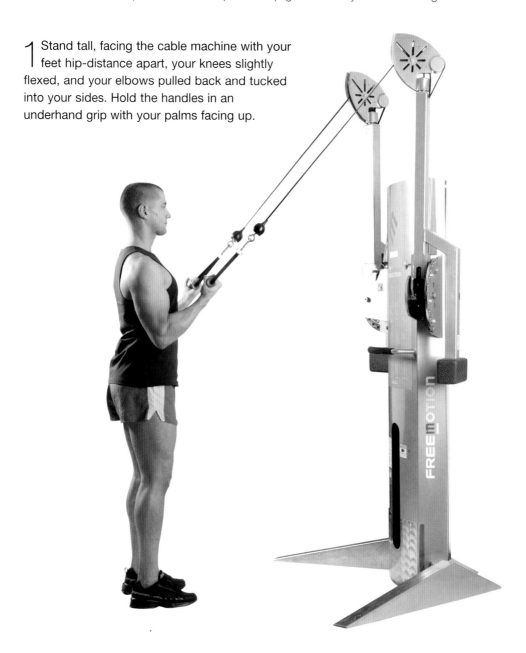

precautions

■ Do not allow your elbows to travel forward during the movement and keep them close in to your sides.
■ Do not allow your torso to flex or your body position to change.
■ Use a lighter weight if you find it difficult to maintain your body position correctly.

2 Inhale slowly, then exhale and extend your arms at the elbow until they are straight. Avoid snapping your arms out and maintain your body position throughout.

3 Inhale, and flex your arms gently at the elbow to return to the starting position.

variation

■ Try the exercise while sitting on a bench or ball.
■ Do the exercise using your arms alternately.
■ Try using different grips (a, b).

a

b
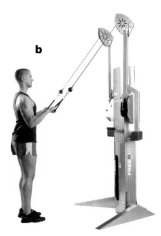

cable triceps overhead extension

intermediate

benefits This exercise is a very good one for developing both the size and shape of the triceps muscles.

1 Position your feet in a split stance—one foot in front of the other with your feet hip-distance apart—facing away from the cable machine. Take an end of the rope in each hand and position it behind your head, with your elbows pointing upward.

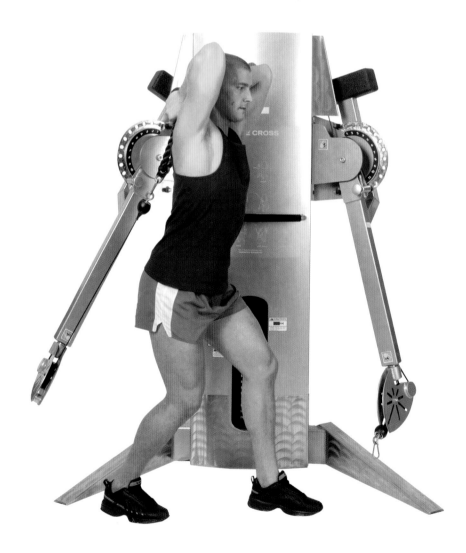

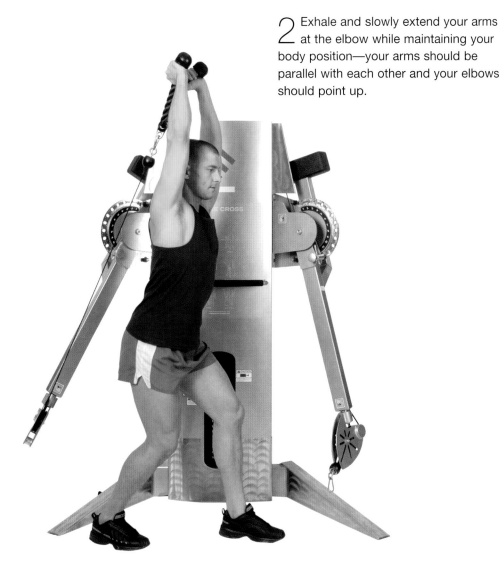

2 Exhale and slowly extend your arms at the elbow while maintaining your body position—your arms should be parallel with each other and your elbows should point up.

3 Keep extending your arms until they are straight, then inhale and slowly lower your arms to return to the starting position.

precautions

■ Start by using a light weight to enable you to become comfortable with the movement.

variation

■ Use a bar attached to the cable instead of a rope.
■ Vary the angle of the cable position.

overhead bar press

intermediate

benefits This exercise helps give the triceps muscles an excellent shape and increased size, and also works the muscles that help stabilize the shoulder.

1 Lie flat on your back on a bench and bring your feet up to the edge of the bench, keeping your feet, knees, and hips in line. Hold the bar above your body with your hands a shoulder-width apart and your elbows, wrists, and shoulders in a vertical line.

2 Inhale and slowly lower the bar toward your forehead by flexing your arms at the elbows—keep your arms parallel to each other and your elbows pointing up.

3 Stop the movement a safe and comfortable distance away from your forehead, then slowly exhale and extend your arms at the elbow to push back to the start position.

variation

- Try the exercise using a ball instead of a bench.
- Use dumbbells instead of a bar.

precautions

- Use a light weight until you become used to the movement.
- Make sure that you take great care as you slowly lower the bar toward your forehead.
- Do not use a heavy weight unless you have a spotter with you.

triceps kickback

intermediate

benefits This exercise is an excellent one for developing triceps, but it is vital that you use the correct technique. Correct body position is especially important.

1 Take a dumbbell in one hand, then place your opposite knee on a bench, together with your other hand, and place your other foot on the floor, flexing it slightly at the knee. Then pull the arm holding the dumbbell straight back and up to your side, making it parallel to the floor—keep your back straight.

2 Holding the dumbbell so that you have a 90° angle at your elbow, exhale slowly and extend your arm as far as it will go, or until your wrist, elbow, and shoulder are in line.

precautions

- Do not swing the dumbbell or use momentum; instead, try to control it throughout the movement.
- If possible, use a mirror to check on your body position.

variation

- Try the exercise without using the bench, but use the same position.

3 Inhale and lower the dumbbell slowly, but only until you reach an angle of 90° at your elbow. Repeat for the required number of reps.

4 Repeat holding the dumbbell in the other hand

chapter 9

legs

- **machine exercises 114–116**
  machine leg curl
  machine leg extension
  machine leg press

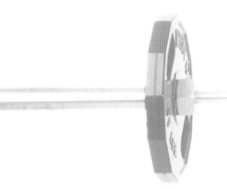

machine leg curl

beginner

benefits This is a basic but effective exercise that promotes the development of the hamstrings.

1 Lay face down on the machine, with its leg pad just above your heels and make sure that your knees line up with its pivot points.

precautions

- Make sure that your starting position feels comfortable.
- Do not move your pelvis or lift it as you pull your heels toward your hips.

variation

- Try doing the exercise using just one leg at a time.
- Experiment with different tempos.

2 Slowly exhale and pull your heels toward your hips, flexing your knees as much as you need to for comfort.

3 When you have moved as far as you can without any sense of straining, inhale and slowly return your heels to the starting position.

machine leg extension

beginner

benefits This is a good basic exercise that develops the quadriceps.

1 Position your lower legs behind the shin pad, making sure that the pad is on the lower part of your shins rather than your ankles. Line your knee up with the pivot points on the machine and make sure that your starting position is comfortable.

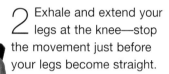

2 Exhale and extend your legs at the knee—stop the movement just before your legs become straight.

3 Inhale and slowly return your legs to the starting position.

precautions

■ Regardless of your tempo, do not kick your legs in any part of the exercise—the movement should remain smooth throughout.
■ Make sure you do not allow the shin pad to leave your legs at any point during the movement.
■ If you experience any pain at all during the course of this exercise stop what you are doing immediately and consult an exercise specialist.

variation

■ Some machines can be adjusted to alter the starting and finishing position if either the movement or the positions are uncomfortable. If you have suffered an injury in the past or feel any pain, try a starting position of 90° at the knee and a finishing position of 160°.
■ In order to correct any differences that there may be in strength between your legs, try doing the exercise using only your weaker leg.

machine leg press

beginner

benefits This is a useful exercise for beginners that develops all the major muscles in the leg, but particularly the quadriceps and the gluteal muscles.

1 Place your feet a hip-distance apart on the footplate with your toes facing forward, and set the seat so that you have a 90° angle at the knee.

precautions

- Make sure that you do not lock your knees as you push out.
- Do not allow your feet to rock on your heels or toes—keep your feet flat and distribute the weight evenly between them.

2 Exhale and slowly push your feet away, making sure that you keep them flat on the footplate.

3 Push out to a point at which you still have a slight amount of flexion at your knees.

4 Inhale and slowly return to the starting position.

variation

- Try the exercise with one leg at a time to correct any imbalance in strength between the two of them.
- When you have mastered the exercise and feel that your legs are becoming stronger, progress to the cable and free-weight leg exercises.
- Vary the position of your feet: try a wide stance and then a narrow one.

cable hamstring curl

intermediate

benefits This exercise not only helps with balance and stability but also develops the strength of your hamstrings. You can work your gluteal muscles if you use the third variation.

1 Stand tall and hold on to the support with both hands, place the foot and ankle of the leg to be exercised into the support strap and raise that leg slightly off the ground. Flex your standing leg slightly at the knee. Your legs should be parallel to each other and your abdominal muscles pulled in—but not so tightly that your breathing is affected.

2 Exhale and slowly pull your ankle up toward your bottom, keeping your hips and knees in line with each other. Do not allow your ankle to travel backward.

3 When your ankle has moved as far as it can, inhale and slowly lower your leg back to the starting position—but do not allow your foot to touch the floor.

4 Repeat for the desired number of repetitions, then repeat the exercise using your other leg.

precautions

- Maintain good posture throughout the exercise and do not allow your pelvis to move.
- Keep the your hip, knee, and foot in line with each other throughout the whole course of the movement.

variation

- Mimic a running motion while you are carrying out the movement.
- As your balance improves, try performing the movement without holding on to the support.
- Hold your leg at 90° at the knee and push back behind you to work more of your gluteal muscles.

cable leg extension

intermediate

benefits This exercise is an excellent one for improving running technique. It requires good balance, but works all of the quadriceps.

1 Stand tall with your planted leg slightly flexed at the knee and your hands on the support bar. Pull in your abdominal muscles slowly, exhale and start to raise your knee.

2 As your knee nears 90° at the hip, slowly extend your lower leg as far as is comfortable without compromising your body position.

3 Inhale, slowly flex your lower leg and return your knee to the starting position—do not allow your foot to touch the ground.

4 Repeat for the desired number of repetitions, then repeat the exercise using your other leg.

precautions

- Maintain good posture throughout the exercise and do not allow your pelvis to move.
- Keep your hip, knee, and foot in line with each other throughout the whole course of the movement.

variation

- Mimic a running motion as you carry out the movement.
- As your balance improves, try to attempt the movement without holding on to the support.
- Just raise your knee without extending your lower leg.

cable front squat

intermediate

benefits This is a slightly more advanced exercise that helps develop balance and stability as well as endowing all the leg muscles, but especially the quadriceps muscles and the gluteals, with considerable strength.

1 Stand tall, a small distance away from the machine, with your feet hip-distance apart and your toes pointing forward. Hold the handles so that your palms are facing each other, and flex your arms fully at the elbow.

variation

- Try squatting with only one leg—but only when your legs have become considerably stronger and you can do the basic exercise extremely well.

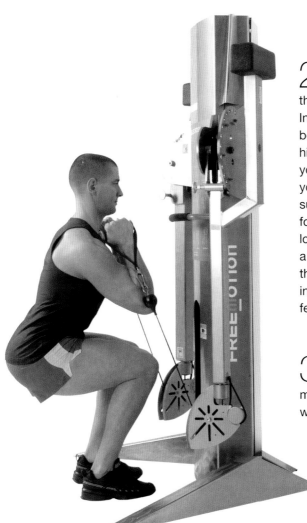

2 Pull in your abdominal muscles, but not so tightly that your breathing is affected. Inhale and slowly lower your body—start the movement at your hips by pushing them out behind you in a sitting motion, then allow your knees to bend, but make sure that they do not travel forward over your toes. Continue lowering your body until you are in a comfortable position but ensure that your knees do not bend inward or bow outward and your feet, knees, and hips are in line.

3 Exhale and slowly push up through your heels, maintaining good posture all the way up through the movement.

precautions

■ Keep your upper body as upright as possible and your back as straight as you can throughout the movement.
■ Keep your shoulders pulled back slightly, being careful not to allow your spine to bend in a hunched position (a).
■ It is vital that you start with a weight that is not too heavy for your arms to hold and allows you to maintain your technique throughout the exercise.

a

dumbbell/barbell lunge

intermediate/advanced

benefits It is not easy to achieve balance and stability during this exercise, but it is nevertheless an extremely good one for developing strength in the legs overall, and especially in the quadriceps and gluteals.

1 Stand tall with your feet hip-distance apart and grasp a dumbbell in each hand with your palms facing inward; make sure that your toes face forward.

precautions

■ Your upper body must remain upright throughout the movement—be careful that you do not bow or twist at any time.

■ Make sure that your body weight drops down and does not transfer forward when your front foot lands.

■ Your front knee must not travel over the toes on your front foot. Keep your feet, knees, and the hips of both legs in line throughout the movement.

■ Do not take too big a stride—try to make sure that your back knee is flexed at 90° when you have lowered it.

■ Technique is vital with this exercise, so use a mirror to monitor your technique whenever possible.

2 Slowly inhale and step one leg forward, keeping your knee above your ankle and dropping the knee of your rear leg toward the floor. Stop the movement when the rear knee is 2 to 3 inches (5 to 7.5 centimeters) from the floor.

3 Exhale and push yourself back to the starting position off your front leg.

4 Repeat for the desired number of repetitions, then repeat the exercise stepping your other leg forward.

variation

- Try using a barbell (a, b, c)—without any weight on the first occasion.
- Lunge onto or off a step.

a

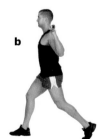

b

c

barbell squat

intermediate/advanced

benefits This exercise is an effective one for developing leg strength and also works the upper-body stabilizing muscles. It requires a reasonable amount of strength and stability.

1 Stand with your feet hip-distance apart and with them facing forward and rest the bar on the back of your shoulders just above your shoulderblades. Pull your abdominal muscles in before starting the movement, but not so tightly that your breathing patterns are affected.

variation

- Vary the position of your feet: use either a wide stance or a narrow one.

2 Inhale slowly and start the movement at your hips by pushing them out behind you in a sitting motion. Then allow your knees to bend, making sure that they do not travel forward over your toes.

precautions

■ Keep your upper body as upright as possible throughout the movement.
■ Do not let your knees travel forward over your toes (a).

a

3 Travel down until your knees are flexed at 90° or at a comfortable point, exhale slowly and push your body weight up through your heels to straighten your legs.

dead lift

advanced

benefits This is a full-body exercise that works all the major muscles in the body, and especially the ones in the legs and back. It is a very difficult exercise to do, but is an excellent strength-developer when it is performed well.

1 Stand with your feet hip-distance apart and bend down in sitting motion until your thighs are parallel to the floor. Keep your back straight and make sure that your spine is as close to the neutral position as possible. Take an overhand grip on the bar with your hands slightly wider than a shoulder-width apart.

2 Exhale, draw your abdominal muscles in, and lift the bar by pushing up through your legs.

3 As the bar reaches your knees during the lift phase, push your hips forward to raise your torso so that you are standing tall with your arms by your sides and the bar resting on your thighs.

4 Hold the position for two seconds, inhale, and return the weight to the floor.

precautions

- The Dead Lift is one of the hardest exercises in this book to do—if you are a beginner or are lacking in confidence, it is important that you consult an exercise specialist before you attempt it.
- To avoid injury, make sure that your back does not become rounded or hunched at any time (a).
- To perfect the exercise, perform a large number of repetitions with a light bar before progressing to a loaded bar.

a

floor exercises

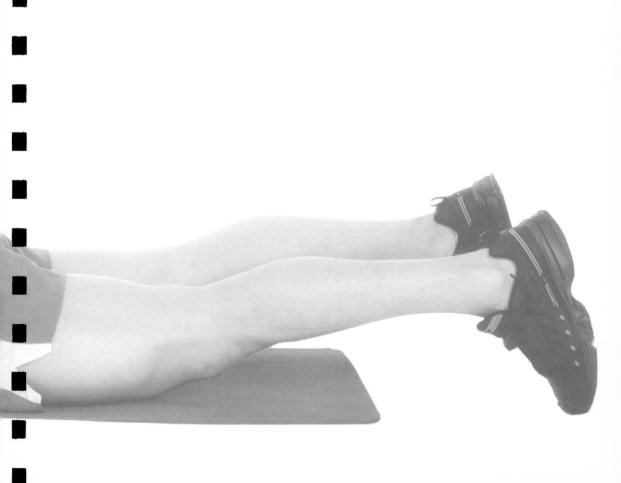

superman

beginner/intermediate

benefits This exercise helps develop core strength and both spinal strength and stability, as well as working the muscles that retract the shoulderblade retractors and the gluteals.

1 Kneel on all fours with your knees under your hips and hip-distance apart and put your hands on the floor a shoulder-width apart under your shoulders. Put your spine into the neutral position. Activate your core by drawing your abdominal muscles back toward your spine.

precautions

■ Do not shift your weight to either side while doing the exercise.
■ Keep your spine in a neutral position and monitor your technique carefully in a mirror if possible.

2 Without any sideways movement and keeping your abdomen pulled in, exhale and slowly raise an opposite arm and leg until they are parallel to the floor—be careful to follow the tempo you have set.

3 Inhale and slowly return your arm and leg to the starting position.

4 Repeat for the desired number of reps, then repeat the exercise using the other arm and leg.

variation

■ If this movement is too difficult, do the exercise with either an arm or a leg alone (a) and build up to using them both at the same time.

■ Try to do single arm or leg raises while balancing on a ball.

a

prone cobra

beginner/intermediate

benefits This exercise helps develop the strength of the spinal muscles and the muscles that retract the shoulderblades, and also improves spinal mobility—it is a useful exercise for anyone who sits at a desk for long periods.

1 Lie face down on the floor with your arms beside your hips and your palms facing up. Activate your core muscles by drawing your abdominals toward your spine and squeezing your gluteals.

2 Slowly exhale and lift your chest off the floor and your arms up and backward toward your hips. Rotate your thumbs toward the ceiling as you carry out the movement.

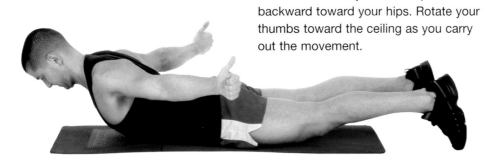

3 Pause at the top of the movement for two seconds, then return to the start position.

variation

- Vary the tempo of the exercise.
- Try doing the exercise when lying on a ball.

precautions

- Make sure that you keep your chin tucked in to your chest
- Do not over-arch your back when you lift your chest.
- Stop immediately if you experience any back pain.

abdominal reverse curl

beginner/intermediate

benefits This exercise works the lower of your abdominal muscles and when performed correctly can eliminate the use of other muscles to cheat the movement.

1 Lie flat on a bench and reach back to hold on to the underside of the bench behind your head. Bend your legs at the knee, raising your feet off the bench so that your knees are over your hips.

2 Slowly draw your abdominal muscles toward your spine, then slowly exhale and push your spine into the bench—start with your lower back and make the movement flow up your spine until your hips roll up off the bench.

4 When you have rolled the full length of your spine, inhale slowly and return to the starting position, pushing your spine into the bench as you roll back down.

3 Imagine that the bench is made of soft plastic and try to leave an imprint of your spine in it.

variation

■ Try doing the exercise on an inclining bench, with your feet lower than your head.
■ Add weight by placing a medicine ball between your knees.

precautions

■ Do not swing your legs to help you gather momentum for the movement.
■ Do not use your arms to help you perform the movement—hold the bench as lightly as you can.

abdominal crunch on a ball

beginner/intermediate

benefits The basic movements of this exercise develop the strength of the abdominal muscles, while the use of the ball helps increase stability.

1 Slowly roll down onto the ball, letting your spine follow its curve, and place your head and neck in a comfortable position on its back. Place your hands at the sides of your head and position your feet hip-distance apart.

2 Draw in your abdominal muscles, then exhale and curl your entire spine up, starting from the neck. Flex at your torso until the distance between the top of your pelvis and the bottom of your ribs stops shortening.

precautions

■ Do not carry your head with your hands.
■ Keep your chin tucked in toward your chest throughout the whole course of the movement.
■ Make sure that the movement is under control and that you flex at your trunk.

variation

■ Experiment with different arm positions.
■ Hold on to a medicine ball (a, b) to increase the difficulty of the exercise.

a

b

chapter 11

programs

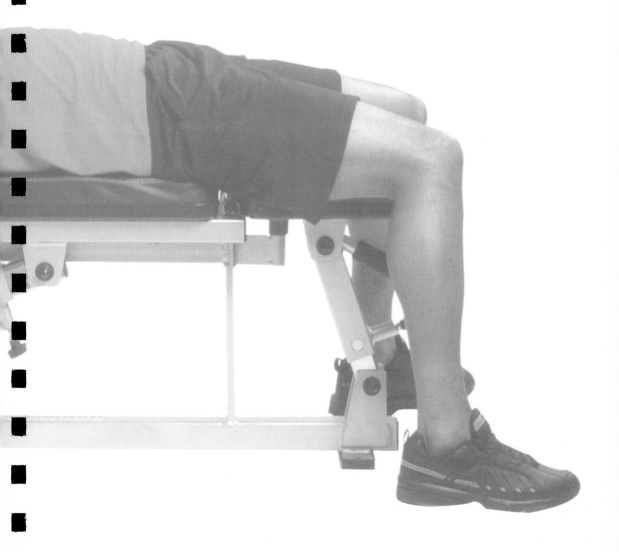

ectomorph exercise routine

beginner

Ectomorphs need sufficient rest periods—a minimum of two minutes—between sets or find that they tire quickly. When you feel that you are growing stronger—this may take two to three months—move on and either construct your own routine or attempt the mesomorph routine (see pages 146–7). As the weight you will be moving will be very heavy it is vital that you do not compromise your exercise technique.

1 hour

exercise		sets	reps	loads	tempo	rest
	Machine chest press **see page 66**	3	6–8	heavy	2:1:2	2–5 minutes
	Machine leg extension **see page 115**	3	6–8	heavy	2:1:2	2–5 minutes
	Machine lateral pull-down **see page 84**	3	6–8	heavy	2:1:2	2–5 minutes
	Cable hamstring curl **see page 117**	3	6–8	heavy	2:1:2	2–5 minutes
	Machine chest flye **see page 67**	3	6–8	heavy	2:1:2	2–5 minutes
	Machine leg press **see page 116**	3	6–8	heavy	2:1:2	2–5 minutes

exercise		sets	reps	loads	tempo	rest
Cable seated low row **see page 82**		3	6–8	heavy	2:1:2	2–5 minutes
Cable front squat **see page 120**		3	6–8	heavy	2:1:2	2–5 minutes
Machine lateral raise **see page 52**		3	6–8	heavy	2:1:2	2–5 minutes
EZ bar standing biceps curl **see page 100**		3	6–8	heavy	2:1:2	2–5 minutes
Machine triceps extension. **see page 104**		3	6–8	heavy	2:1:2	2–5 minutes
Abdominal reverse curl **see page 133**		3	12–15	body weight	4:2:4	1 minute
Superman **see page 130**		3	12–15	body weight	4:2:4	1 minute

developing strength and increasing muscle mass (a)

beginner

It is important that a beginner adheres strictly to this routine and does not leave out any exercises—doing so could cause muscle imbalance problems that could lead to postural problems and, possibly, injury. The routine will allow you to maximize your development and enable you to progress to a harder pre-planned routine, such as the one on pages 142–3, or one you construct yourself. Start slowly and allow yourself at least eight weeks before you move on.

1 hour

exercise		sets	reps	loads	tempo	rest
	Cable chest press **see page 70**	3	8–12	moderate	2:1:2	30 seconds– 1 minute
	Machine leg extension **see page 115**	3	8–12	moderate	2:1:2	30 seconds– 1 minute
	Cable seated low row **see page 82**	3	8–12	moderate	2:1:2	30 seconds– 1 minute
	Machine leg curl **see page 114**	3	8–12	moderate	2:1:2	30 seconds– 1 minute

exercise	sets	reps	loads	tempo	rest
Machine shoulder press **see page 50**	3	8–12	moderate	2:1:2	30 seconds–1 minute
Machine leg press **see page 116**	3	8–12	moderate	2:1:2	30 seconds–1 minute
Preacher bench biceps curl **see page 94**	3	8–12	moderate	2:1:2	30 seconds–1 minute
Machine triceps extension **see page 104**	3	8–12	moderate	2:1:2	30 seconds–1 minute
Abdominal crunch on a ball **see page 134**	3	8–12	body weight	4:2:4	30 seconds–1 minute
Prone cobra **see page 132**	3	8–12	body weight	4:2:4	30 seconds–1 minute

developing strength and increasing muscle mass (b)

beginner

This routine should only be attempted if you have previous experience of resistance training or you have a reasonable level of fitness. It comprises predominately machine exercises, so if you want to develop it further after you have adapted to it you can replace the machine exercises with cable or free-weight exercises for the same muscle group— for example, you could replace machine chest presses with cable chest presses.

1 hour

exercise	sets	reps	loads	tempo	rest
Machine chest press **see page 66**	3	8–12	moderate	2:1:2	30 seconds– 1 minute
Cable seated low row **see page 82**	3	8–12	moderate	2:1:2	30 seconds– 1 minute
Machine chest flye **see page 67**	3	8–12	moderate	2:1:2	30 seconds– 1 minute
Assisted pull-up **see page 80**	3	8–12	moderate	2:1:2	30 seconds– 1 minute

exercise	sets	reps	loads	tempo	rest
Machine leg press **see page 116**	3	8–12	moderate	2:1:2	30 seconds– 1 minute
Machine lateral raise **see page 52**	3	8–12	moderate	2:1:2	30 seconds– 1 minute
Triceps assisted dip **see page 105**	3	8–12	moderate	2:1:2	30 seconds– 1 minute
Dumbbell biceps curl **see page 98**	3	8–12	moderate	2:1:2	30 seconds– 1 minute
Abdominal crunch on a ball **see page 134**	3	12–15	body weight	4:2:4	30 seconds– 1 minute
Superman, variation (a) **see page 131**	3	12–15	body weight	4:2:4	30 seconds– 1 minute

circuit routine

beginner

If you are a beginner, attempt this full-body circuit only if you have a high base level of fitness. The aim of this routine is it to work all the muscle groups, with minimum rest and maximum output. A routine such as this can overload not only the muscles but the cardiovascular system—though it burns a large number of calories. It is a very effective workout in terms of time, too.

1 hour

exercise		sets	reps	loads	tempo	rest
	Dumbbell/ barbell lunge **see page 122**	3–5	15–30	light to moderate	2:1:2	No rest until all 10 exercises have been completed
	Barbell bench press **see page 74**	3–5	15–30	light to moderate	2:1:2	No rest until all 10 exercises have been completed
	Bar bent row **see page 90**	3–5	15–30	light to moderate	2:1:2	No rest until all 10 exercises have been completed
	Bar military press **see page 60**	3–5	15–30	light to moderate	2:1:2	No rest until all 10 exercises have been completed

exercise	sets	reps	loads	tempo	rest
Dumbbell biceps curl **see page 98**	3–5	15–30	light to moderate	2:1:2	No rest until all 10 exercises have been completed
Bar upright row **see page 61**	3–5	15–30	light to moderate	2:1:2	No rest until all 10 exercises have been completed
Barbell squat **see page 124**	3–5	15–30	light to moderate	2:1:2	No rest until all 10 exercises have been completed
Overhead bar press **see page 110**	3–5	15–30	light to moderate	4:2:4	No rest until all 10 exercises have been completed
Abdominal reverse curl **see page 133**	3–5	15–30	light to moderate	4:2:4	No rest until all 10 exercises have been completed
Prone cobra **see page 132**	3–5	15–30	light to moderate	4:2:4	then a recovery period of 2–3 minutes

mesomorph exercise routine

intermediate

If you are a mesomorph you tend to be a "fast gainer" (see body types, page 26) and will adapt quickly to an exercise routine, so a more advanced routine such as this suits you. At first you may need to keep the rest periods slightly on the high side in order to recover sufficiently for the next set. When you start to exceed 12 repetitions for each of your three sets increase the weight, but make sure that you retain good form and technique. If you are unsure of what tempo to use, refer back to the tempo section (see page 34), making sure that you follow the routine carefully in order to achieve the best results.

1 hour

exercise		sets	reps	loads	tempo	rest
	Cable chest press **see page 70**	3	8–12	moderate	2:1:2	30 seconds– 1.5 minutes
	Cable front squat **see page 120**	3	8–12	moderate	2:1:2	30 seconds– 1.5 minutes
	Assisted pull-up **see page 80**	3	8–12	moderate	2:1:2	30 seconds– 1.5 minutes
	Dead lift **see page 126**	3	8–12	moderate	2:1:2	30 seconds– 1.5 minutes

exercise		sets	reps	loads	tempo	rest
Bar military press **see page 60**		3	8–12	moderate	2:1:2	30 seconds–1 minute
Standing cable biceps curl **see page 95**		3	8–12	moderate	2:1:2	30 seconds–1 minute
Triceps assisted dip **see page 105**		3	8–12	moderate	2:1:2	30 seconds–1 minute
Abdominal crunch on a ball **see page 134**		3	12–15	body weight	4:2:4	30 seconds–1 minute
Abdominal reverse curl **see page 133**		3	12–15	body weight	4:2:4	30 seconds–1 minute
Prone cobra **see page 132**		3	10	body weight	4:2:4	30 seconds–1 minute

endomorph exercise routine

intermediate

Supersets (see page 25) are good for endomorphs as they benefit from high-intensity exercise. Do one set of the first two exercises back to back, rest for one minute, then do the second and third sets. The "tempo" figures below refer to the number of seconds spent in the three phases of movement, for example "3:1:3" means 3 seconds in the concentric phase, 1 second in the isometric phase, and 3 seconds in the eccentric phase.

1 hour

exercise		sets	reps	loads	tempo	rest
	Cable chest press **see page 70**	3	12–15	light to moderate	3:1:3	1 minute
	Cable chest flye **see page 72**	3	12–15	light to moderate	3:1:3	
	Machine leg extension **see page 115**	3	12–15	light to moderate	3:1:3	1 minute
	Machine leg curl **see page 114**	3	12–15	light to moderate	3:1:3	
	Cable seated low row **see page 82**	3	12–15	light to moderate	3:1:3	1 minute
	Machine lateral pull-down **see page 84**	3	12–15	light to moderate	3:1:3	

exercise		sets	reps	loads	tempo	rest
Cable front squat see page 120		3	12–15	light to moderate	3:1:3	1 minute
Machine lateral raise see page 52		3	12–15	light to moderate	3:1:3	
Dumbbell biceps curl (hammer grip) see page 98		3	12–15	light to moderate	3:1:3	1 minute
Preacher bench biceps curl see page 94		3	12–15	light to moderate	3:1:3	
Machine triceps extension see page 104		3	12–15	light to moderate	3:1:3	1 minute
Cable triceps push-down see page 106		3	12–15	light to moderate	3:1:3	
Abdominal crunch on a ball see page 134		3	12–15	body weight	4:2:4	1 minute
Prone cobra see page 132		3	10	body weight	4:2:4	

split routine

intermediate

Intermediates may appreciate the variety that a split routine offers. It should be performed over two days, with the third day off and the routine starting again on the fourth day. So, for example:

Monday   – chest, shoulders, and triceps exercises
Tuesday   – back, legs, and biceps exercises
Wednesday   – a rest day
Thursday   – chest, shoulders, and triceps exercises
Friday   – back, legs, and biceps exercises
Saturday   – a rest day
Sunday   – a rest day

1–1½ hours per day

Day 1: Chest, Shoulders, and Triceps

exercise		sets	reps	loads	tempo	rest
	Barbell bench press see page 74	3–6	6–12	moderate to heavy	2:1:2	30 seconds–1.5 minutes
	Dumbbell flye see page 76	3–6	6–12	moderate	2:1:2	30 seconds–1.5 minutes
	Cable crossover see page 68	3–6	6–12	moderate	2:1:2	30 seconds–1.5 minutes

exercise		sets	reps	loads	tempo	rest
	Bar military press variation **see page 60**	3–6	6–12	moderate to heavy	2:1:2	30 seconds– 1.5 minutes
	Dumbbell lateral raise **see page 62**	3–6	6–12	moderate	2:1:2	30 seconds– 1.5 minutes
	Bar upright row **see page 61**	3	6–12	moderate to heavy	2:1:2	30 seconds– 1.5 minutes
	Cable rear lateral raise **see page 54**	3	6–12	moderate	2:1:2	30 seconds– 1.5 minutes
	Cable triceps overhead extension **see page 108**	3	6–12	moderate to heavy	2:1:2	30 seconds– 1.5 minutes

Day 2: Back, Legs, and Biceps

exercise		sets	reps	loads	tempo	rest
	Bar bent row **see page 90**	3–6	6–12	moderate to heavy	2:1:2	30 seconds–1.5 minutes
	Cable seated low row **see page 82**	3–6	6–12	moderate to heavy	2:1:2	30 seconds–1.5 minutes
	Cable straight arm pull-down **see page 86**	3–6	6–12	moderate	2:1:2	30 seconds–1.5 minutes
	Barbell squat **see page 124**	3–6	6–12	moderate to heavy	2:1:2	30 seconds–1.5 minutes
	Machine leg extension **see page 115**	3–6	6–12	moderate	2:1:2	30 seconds–1.5 minutes

exercise		sets	reps	loads	tempo	rest
Machine leg curl see page 114		3–6	6–12	moderate	2:1:2	30 seconds– 1.5 minutes
Dead lift see page 126		3–6	6–12	moderate to heavy	2:1:2	30 seconds– 1.5 minutes
Dumbbell biceps curl see page 98		3–6	6–12	moderate	2:1:2	30 seconds– 1.5 minutes
EZ bar standing biceps curl see page 100		3–6	6–12	moderate to heavy	2:1:2	30 seconds– 1.5 minutes
Abdominal reverse crunch see page 133		3–6	12–20	N/A	2:1:2	30–45 seconds
Abdominal crunch on a ball see page 134		3–6	12–20	N/A	2:1:2	30–45 seconds

developing strength and increasing muscle mass (c)

intermediate

This routine is designed for those who have some experience of resistance training. The exercises it sets are more complex than those that are suitable for beginners and require more concentration on technique. Make sure that you take sufficient rest between exercises when you first start on this routine and do not increase the weight until you can perform them efficiently. If possible, use mirrors to monitor your technique.

1 hour

exercise	sets	reps	loads	tempo	rest
Barbell squat **see page 124**	4–5	10–12	moderate	2:2:2	60 seconds
Dumbbell/ barbell lunge **see page 122**	4–5	10–12	moderate	2:2:2	60 seconds
Bar bent row **see page 90**	4–5	10–12	moderate	2:2:2	60 seconds
Bar military press **see page 60**	4–5	10–12	moderate	2:2:2	60 seconds
Cable side lateral raise **see page 53**	2–3	12–15	moderate	2:2:2	60 seconds
Cable crossover **see page 68**	2–3	12–15	moderate	2:2:2	60 seconds

exercise		sets	reps	loads	tempo	rest
Barbell bench press **see page 74**		4–5	10–12	moderate	2:2:2	60 seconds
Cable triceps overhead extension **see page 108**		4–5	10–12	moderate	2:2:2	60 seconds
Standing cable biceps curl **see page 95**		4–5	10–12	light to moderate	2:2:2	60 seconds
Rotator cuff internal **see page 56**		2–3	12–15	moderate	3:2:3	45 seconds
Abdominal crunch on a ball **see page 134**		2–3	15–30	n/a	2:1:2	45 seconds
Abdominal reverse curl **see page 133**		2–3	12–15	n/a	2:1:2	45 seconds
Prone cobra **see page 132**		3–4	12–15	n/a	2:1:2	45 seconds

superset routine

intermediate

Supersets (see page 25) offer routines that work two or more parts of the body in quick succession, so this program should be performed with no rest between exercises, and with a quick tempo throughout. For example: Do the barbell bench presses then go straight into the assisted pull-ups, then rest for 60 seconds before repeating.

The rest period can be between 30 and 60 seconds before moving to the next superset.

1–1$\frac{1}{2}$ hours

exercise	sets	reps	loads	tempo	rest
Barbell bench press see page 74					
Assisted pull-up see page 80	2–3	10–15	moderate	1:1:1	none
Bar military press see page 60					
Bar upright row see page 61	2–3	10–15	moderate	1:1:1	none

exercise	sets	reps	loads	tempo	rest
Cable front squat **see page 120**					
	2–3	10–15	moderate	1:1:1	none
Machine leg curl **see page 114**					
Dumbbell biceps curl **see page 98**					
	2–3	10–15	moderate	1:1:1	none
Triceps assisted dip **see page 105**					
Abdominal reverse curl **see page 133**					
	2–3	10–15	body weight	1:1:1	none
Prone cobra **see page 132**					

index